How Racism Has Changed the World

Can We Fight It Together?

Dr Bhaskar Bora

1

Table of Contents

Prologue

Racism is an insidious force that has shaped societies across the globe for centuries. It is a deep-seated problem that affects millions of lives in profound and often devastating ways. Understanding how racism has changed the world is not only about recognizing the historical and contemporary manifestations of racial discrimination but also about exploring the resilience, resistance, and contributions of marginalized communities.

This book, "How Racism Has Changed the World," is a journey through time and across continents. It delves into the roots of racism, examines its various forms, and highlights the enduring impact it has had on different cultures and societies. By looking at the United States, the United Kingdom, and other countries, we can see both the unique and universal aspects of this pervasive issue.

A Personal Journey

For me, this exploration is deeply personal. As someone who has experienced the sting of racism and witnessed its effects on others, I felt compelled to write this book. My own encounters with discrimination, along with the stories shared by friends, colleagues, and strangers, have shaped my understanding and fuelled my passion for change. Writing this book is my way of contributing to the ongoing struggle for equality and justice.

The Purpose of This Book

The purpose of this book is threefold. First, it aims to educate by providing a comprehensive overview of the history and present-day realities of racism. Second, it seeks to inspire by sharing stories of resilience, resistance, and the fight for justice. Lastly, it calls readers to action, encouraging each of us to play our part in dismantling racism and building a more equitable world.

A Global Perspective

Racism is not confined to any one country or culture. Its manifestations and impacts can be seen worldwide, from the transatlantic slave trade to apartheid in South Africa, from the caste system in India to the treatment of indigenous peoples in Australia and the Americas. By examining these different contexts, we can gain a deeper understanding of how racism operates and how it can be challenged.

The Structure of This Book

This book is divided into fifteen chapters, each focusing on a different aspect of racism. We begin with a historical overview, tracing the origins of racial discrimination and its evolution over time. We then move to specific case studies, looking at how racism has affected the United States, the United Kingdom, and other countries. We explore the different forms of racism, including institutional and hidden racism, and examine the impact of racism on various cultures.

Throughout the book, we highlight stories of individuals and communities who have stood up against injustice and worked tirelessly for change. These narratives remind us that while racism is a powerful force, it is not insurmountable. Human resilience and the desire for justice can and do make a difference.

A Call to Action

As you read this book, I hope you will not only gain a deeper understanding of racism but also feel inspired to take action. Whether through educating yourself and others, supporting anti-racist organizations, advocating for policy changes, or challenging racism in your daily life, every effort counts.

The journey towards racial equality is long and arduous, but it is one we must undertake together. By acknowledging the past, understanding the present, and committing to change, we can build a future where everyone, regardless of their race or ethnicity, is treated with dignity and respect.

Thank you for joining me on this journey. Let us move forward with determination and hope, knowing that together, we can create a more just and equitable world.

Dr Bhaskar Bora

Chapter 1: Introduction - A Personal Journey

As a first-generation immigrant, I was acutely aware of the differences that marked me as 'other' in the eyes of those around me. Born into a society that prided itself on diversity, I often found myself navigating the unspoken rules and biases that came with my skin colour and ethnic background. My journey, like that of many others, is a tapestry woven with experiences of subtle exclusions and overt hostilities, yet also resilience and hope.

I remember my first encounter with racism vividly. As a new migrant Doctor from India, I moved to a new neighbourhood in England where my family was one of the few non-white residents. The initial excitement of new surroundings quickly faded as I realized that my presence was often met with suspicious glances and whispered conversations.

As time passed, these experiences did not disappear; they merely evolved. Working in the NHS, I encountered institutional racism for the first time. Despite my qualifications and hard work, I noticed a consistent pattern of being overlooked for opportunities that seemed readily available to my peers. The subtlety of this discrimination made it even more insidious—there were no explicit slurs or outright denials, just a persistent, pervasive sense that I was always a step behind, forever trying to catch up. I must however, say that it was not the NHS itself but some people withing the institution that made me feel I did.

It was during these formative years that I began to delve deeper into the history and mechanisms of racism. I learned about the pseudo-scientific theories of the Enlightenment era that classified humans into rigid racial hierarchies, justifying the exploitation and subjugation of entire populations. These theories, once cloaked in the language of science, laid the groundwork for centuries of systemic oppression. Understanding this history was a revelation; it connected the dots between my personal experiences and the broader societal patterns.

One particularly poignant moment was when I visited a former slave plantation in the southern United States. Walking through the grounds, I felt the weight of history pressing down on me—the echoes of suffering and resilience resonating through the centuries. The experience was both harrowing and enlightening. It brought into sharp focus the enduring legacy of slavery and how its tentacles still grip our present, shaping racial dynamics and inequalities.

In my professional life, the challenges of racism persisted, albeit in more nuanced forms. As a doctor, I witnessed firsthand how racial biases could influence patient care and outcomes. Studies have shown that minority patients often receive less effective pain management and are less likely to be given life-saving treatments compared to their white counterparts. These disparities are not merely statistical anomalies; they are real, lived experiences that underscore the urgent need for systemic change.

Through my personal and professional journey, I have encountered many individuals who, despite facing similar challenges, have managed to carve out spaces of resistance and empowerment. Their stories of perseverance and triumph in the face of adversity are a testament to the human spirit's indomitable will. It is these stories that inspire me to write this book, to shed light on the pervasive issue of racism, and to explore its multifaceted impact on our world.

This book is not just an academic exercise; it is a call to action. By understanding the historical roots and contemporary manifestations of racism, we can begin to dismantle the structures that perpetuate it. We must recognize that racism is not a problem confined to the past; it is a present-day reality that demands our attention and action.

As we embark on this journey together, I invite you to reflect on your own experiences and the ways in which racism has touched your life or the lives of those around you. Let us move forward with a commitment to empathy, understanding, and, most importantly, change. For it is only through collective effort that we can hope to build a world where every individual, regardless of their race, can live with dignity and equality.

The more I explored the history of racism, the more I realized that it wasn't just a series of isolated incidents or individual prejudices. Racism is a complex, systemic issue that has been ingrained in the fabric of societies across the world. Understanding this helped me see my experiences in a broader context and recognize the patterns that perpetuate racial inequality.

One of the most striking realizations was how deeply entrenched racism is in the very institutions that are supposed to protect and serve us. For instance, the education system, which is meant to be a great equalizer, often reinforces racial disparities. Studies have shown that minority students are more likely to attend underfunded schools, face harsher disciplinary actions, and have lower graduation rates compared to their white peers. These disparities are not just a result of individual prejudices but are embedded in the policies and practices that govern our educational institutions.

Similarly, in the healthcare system, racial biases can have life-or-death consequences. Research has demonstrated that black women are more likely to die during childbirth than white women, even when accounting for socioeconomic status and access to healthcare. These disparities are a stark reminder that racism is not just a social issue but a public health crisis that demands urgent attention.

In the workplace, racial discrimination can manifest in various forms, from hiring practices to career advancement opportunities. Despite equal qualifications, minority candidates often find themselves passed over for jobs or promotions, leading to significant income disparities over time. This not only affects individuals but also contributes to the broader economic inequality that persists in our society.

Throughout my journey, I have also witnessed the psychological toll that racism takes on individuals. The constant need to prove oneself, the fear of being judged or mistreated based on one's race, and the internalization of negative stereotypes can lead to chronic stress, anxiety, and other mental health issues. The emotional burden of racism is something that many people of colour carry with them daily, often in silence.

Despite these challenges, there are countless stories of resilience and resistance. Communities of colour have always found ways to fight back against oppression and build networks of support and solidarity. From the civil rights movements in the United States to the anti-apartheid struggle in South Africa, history is replete with examples of collective action and perseverance in the face of overwhelming odds.

These stories of resistance are not just historical footnotes; they continue to inspire and inform current movements for racial justice. The Black Lives Matter movement, for example, has brought renewed attention to issues of police brutality and systemic racism, sparking global protests and calls for reform. Similarly, indigenous communities around the world are fighting to protect their lands and rights, challenging the legacies of colonialism and exploitation.

In writing this book, my goal is to shine a light on these struggles and highlight the interconnectedness of our fight against racism. It is a fight that requires all of us to examine our own biases, challenge the status quo, and work towards a more just and equitable world. Racism is not an intractable problem; it is a human-made system that can be dismantled through collective effort and solidarity.

As we move forward, I invite you to join me in this journey of exploration and action. Let us commit to learning, unlearning, and relearning, to listening to those most affected by racism, and to taking concrete steps towards change. Together, we can create a world where everyone, regardless of their race, can thrive.

Reflecting on my personal experiences and the broader societal patterns of racism, it becomes evident that education plays a crucial role in both perpetuating and challenging these dynamics. From early childhood, the stories we are told and the history we are taught shape our understanding of race and identity. Unfortunately, much of this education has been historically skewed, often omitting or misrepresenting the experiences of people of colour.

In school, the curriculum predominantly centred around the achievements and perspectives of white individuals, with little to no mention of the contributions and struggles of other racial groups. This lack of representation not only marginalizes these groups but also reinforces a narrow worldview that privileges whiteness. For many students of colour, this erasure can be disheartening and alienating, leading to a sense of invisibility and disconnection from their own heritage. However, education also holds the potential to be a powerful tool for change. By incorporating diverse perspectives and fostering critical thinking, we can challenge the dominant narratives and promote a more inclusive understanding of history and society. This requires a concerted effort to diversify curricula, train educators on issues of race and bias, and create learning environments that celebrate and respect all cultures.

The importance of representation extends beyond the classroom. In media, literature, and popular culture, the portrayal of different races significantly influences public perception and societal attitudes. Historically, these portrayals have often been stereotypical and reductive, perpetuating harmful myths and biases. For example, the depiction of African Americans as criminals or Latinos as illegal immigrants reinforces negative stereotypes that fuel discrimination and violence.

Progress is being made, albeit slowly. There are increasing efforts to amplify the voices and stories of marginalized communities in media and entertainment. Films, books, and television shows that centre on the experiences of people of colour are gaining recognition and acclaim, challenging audiences to confront their own prejudices and expand their horizons. These cultural shifts are vital in the broader fight against racism, as they help to humanize and validate the experiences of those who have been historically marginalized.

As individuals, we also have a role to play in this cultural shift. By actively seeking out and supporting diverse voices, we can contribute to a more equitable and inclusive society. This means reading books by authors of colour, watching films and shows that highlight different perspectives, and engaging in conversations about race and representation. It is through these small, everyday actions that we can begin to dismantle the systemic biases that permeate our culture.

Throughout my life, I have found solace and strength in the stories of others who have faced and overcome similar challenges. Their resilience and courage in the face of adversity have been a source of inspiration and a reminder that we are not alone in this fight. By sharing our stories and listening to the stories of others, we can build a sense of community and solidarity that is essential for meaningful change.

In this book, I aim to weave together these personal narratives with historical analysis and contemporary reflections to provide a comprehensive understanding of racism and its impact. By examining the past, we can better understand the present and work towards a more just future. This journey requires honesty, empathy, and a willingness to confront uncomfortable truths, but it is a journey we must undertake if we are to create a world where everyone is treated with dignity and respect.

As we continue to explore the multifaceted issue of racism, I encourage you to reflect on your own experiences and consider how they fit into the larger narrative. What role can you play in challenging racism and promoting equity? How can you support and uplift the voices of those who have been marginalized? Together, we can make a difference, one story, one action at a time.

As I delve deeper into the multifaceted nature of racism, it becomes increasingly clear that this issue cannot be addressed in isolation. Racism intersects with various other forms of discrimination, such as sexism, classism, and homophobia, creating complex layers of oppression that many individuals navigate daily. These intersections must be acknowledged and understood to fully grasp the pervasive impact of racism.

For instance, women of colour often face unique challenges that stem from both racial and gender discrimination. The concept of intersectionality, introduced by scholar Kimberlé Crenshaw, highlights how overlapping identities can compound experiences of oppression. Understanding intersectionality is crucial for developing comprehensive strategies to combat racism and promote social justice.

One area where intersectionality is particularly evident is in the workplace. Women of colour often encounter a "double jeopardy" of biases, making it harder for them to advance in their careers compared to their white or male counterparts. They might face stereotypes that paint them as less competent or too aggressive, and these biases can influence hiring decisions, promotions, and workplace dynamics. Addressing these issues requires targeted efforts to create inclusive and equitable work environments that recognize and value diversity in all its forms.

In addition to gender, socio-economic status plays a significant role in shaping individuals' experiences with racism. Economic inequality is both a cause and a consequence of racial discrimination. Historically marginalized communities often have less access to quality education, healthcare, and job opportunities, perpetuating a cycle of poverty and exclusion. Tackling racism thus involves addressing broader issues of economic justice and ensuring that all individuals have the resources and opportunities to succeed.

Moreover, the intersection of racism and homophobia affects LGBTQ+ individuals of colour in distinct ways. They may face rejection and violence within their own communities as well as from the broader society, leading to heightened vulnerability and marginalization. Advocacy and support networks that address the specific needs of LGBTQ+ people of colour are essential in creating a more inclusive and supportive society.

Throughout my journey, I have been fortunate to meet and collaborate with individuals and organizations dedicated to fighting these intersecting forms of discrimination. Their work has shown me the importance of solidarity and allyship in the struggle for justice. By standing together and recognizing the interconnectedness of our struggles, we can build stronger and more effective movements for change.

Another critical aspect of understanding and combating racism is recognizing the role of privilege. Privilege, in this context, refers to the unearned advantages that individuals have by virtue of their race, gender, class, or other characteristics. Acknowledging privilege is not about inducing guilt but about understanding how systemic inequalities benefit some while disadvantaging others. It is a crucial step towards creating a more equitable society.

For those who hold privilege, becoming an ally involves listening to and amplifying the voices of marginalized communities, challenging discriminatory practices, and using their influence to advocate for change. Allies play a vital role in the fight against racism, as their support can help dismantle barriers and create opportunities for those who have been historically excluded.

Education is a powerful tool in this regard. By educating ourselves and others about the realities of racism and the importance of allyship, we can foster greater empathy and understanding. Workshops, seminars, and discussions about race and privilege can be transformative, encouraging individuals to reflect on their own biases and take meaningful action.

As we continue this journey together, I invite you to consider how intersectionality and privilege shape your experiences and those of others around you. Reflect on the ways in which you can contribute to the fight against racism, both in your personal life and within your community. It is only through collective effort and a commitment to justice that we can hope to create a world where everyone, regardless of their race or identity, can live with dignity and equality.

One of the most profound realizations in my journey has been the understanding that racism is not just an individual failing, but a systemic issue embedded in our institutions, cultures, and policies. This systemic nature of racism means that it operates independently of individual intent, often perpetuating inequality even in the absence of overt prejudice.

Consider the criminal justice system, where racial disparities are stark and persistent. People of colour, particularly Black and Latino individuals, are disproportionately targeted by law enforcement, face harsher sentencing, and are overrepresented in the prison population. These disparities are not merely the result of individual biases but are deeply rooted in policies and practices that discriminate against marginalized communities. The war on drugs, for instance, has disproportionately affected Black communities, leading to mass incarceration and long-term socio-economic consequences.

Education, too, reflects these systemic issues. Minority students often attend under-resourced schools with fewer opportunities and lower expectations. This educational inequity sets the stage for lifelong disparities in employment, income, and social mobility. The achievement gap between white students and students of colour is a symptom of broader systemic issues, including residential segregation, funding inequalities, and implicit biases within the education system.

Healthcare disparities are another clear example of systemic racism. Studies consistently show that racial and ethnic minorities receive lower-quality care compared to their white counterparts, leading to worse health outcomes. Factors such as implicit bias among healthcare providers, socio-economic barriers, and historical mistrust of the medical system contribute to these disparities. The COVID-19 pandemic has further highlighted these inequalities, with communities of colour experiencing higher infection and mortality rates.

Housing policies have also played a significant role in perpetuating racial inequality. Practices like redlining, where banks and insurers denied services to residents in certain areas based on racial composition, have had long-lasting impacts on wealth accumulation and neighborhood development. Even today, people of colour are more likely to live in neighborhoods with fewer resources and higher levels of pollution and crime.

Understanding the systemic nature of racism is crucial because it shifts the focus from individual prejudices to structural change. While challenging personal biases is important, dismantling racism requires addressing the policies and practices that sustain inequality. This involves advocating for fairer laws, equitable resource distribution, and inclusive institutions that serve all members of society.

Throughout my life, I have witnessed the power of grassroots movements and community organizing in driving systemic change. The civil rights movement, led by figures like Martin Luther King Jr. and Malcolm X, brought about significant legislative changes, such as the Civil Rights Act and the Voting Rights Act. More recently, movements like Black Lives Matter have mobilized millions around the world to demand justice and accountability for racial violence and systemic discrimination.

These movements remind us that change is possible but requires sustained effort and solidarity. Allies from all walks of life must come together to support these efforts, leveraging their privilege and platforms to amplify marginalized voices and advocate for justice. It is through collective action that we can hope to dismantle the structures of racism and build a more equitable society.

As we conclude this introductory chapter, I want to emphasize the importance of hope and perseverance. The fight against racism is challenging and often disheartening, but it is also filled with moments of triumph and progress. By learning from the past, listening to those most affected, and committing to continuous action, we can create meaningful change.

This book is a call to action, a plea for understanding, and a roadmap for those who wish to join the fight against racism. Together, we can build a world where everyone, regardless of their race, has the opportunity to thrive. Let us embark on this journey with open hearts and minds, ready to challenge the status quo and work towards a brighter, more inclusive future.

Chapter 2: The History of Racism

To truly understand the present landscape of racism, we must first delve into its historical roots. Racism, as we know it today, is not a recent phenomenon but has evolved over centuries, shaped by economic, social, and political forces. This chapter will trace the origins of racial discrimination, exploring how it became institutionalized and perpetuated across different eras and societies.

The concept of race, and by extension racism, has ancient origins. In ancient civilizations like Greece and Rome, distinctions were often made based on ethnicity and cultural differences. However, these distinctions were not necessarily rooted in the same ideas of inherent superiority or inferiority that characterize modern racism. In these societies, the concept of "barbarian" was used to denote those who were outside the Greek or Roman cultural sphere, often seen as uncivilized or inferior. Yet, this did not translate directly into the racial hierarchies that emerged later.

The turning point came during the Age of Exploration and the subsequent colonization of the Americas, Africa, and Asia. European explorers and colonizers encountered diverse populations and driven by economic motives and a desire for domination, began to develop pseudo-scientific theories to justify their actions. The idea of race as a biological determinant of human abilities and worth gained traction, providing a convenient rationale for slavery, exploitation, and genocide.

One of the most influential periods in the development of modern racism was the Enlightenment. Paradoxically, this era, which championed reason, science, and progress, also saw the rise of racial theories that classified humanity into hierarchical categories. Thinkers like Carl Linnaeus and Johann Friedrich Blumenbach contributed to the classification of humans into distinct races, often placing Europeans at the top of this hierarchy. These classifications were not just academic exercises but had real-world implications, influencing laws and policies that discriminated against non-European peoples.

The transatlantic slave trade, which began in the 15th century and lasted for over 400 years, is a glaring example of how these racial theories were put into practice. Millions of Africans were forcibly taken from their homelands and subjected to brutal conditions in the Americas. The dehumanization of Africans was justified by a belief in their supposed racial inferiority. This not only facilitated the economic exploitation of enslaved people but also entrenched a racial divide that has persisted for centuries.

In the Americas, the legacy of slavery is deeply embedded in the social and economic fabric. After the abolition of slavery, systems like Jim Crow laws in the United States continued to enforce racial segregation and discrimination. These laws, which were in place from the late 19th century until the mid-20th century, institutionalized racism and perpetuated inequalities that are still felt today. The civil rights movement of the 1960s was a pivotal moment in challenging these injustices, but the struggle for racial equality continues.

Racism was not confined to the Americas. In Europe, colonialism had a profound impact on racial attitudes and policies. The British Empire, at its height, ruled over vast territories in Africa, Asia, and the Caribbean. Colonial rule was often justified by a belief in the superiority of the British race and the supposed benefits of bringing "civilization" to the "uncivilized" parts of the world. This paternalistic view masked the exploitation and oppression that characterized colonial rule, leaving a lasting legacy of racial inequality in many former colonies.

In Asia, countries like India experienced racism through British colonial rule. The British employed a strategy of divide and rule, exacerbating ethnic and religious tensions to maintain control. This not only led to social divisions but also reinforced the idea of racial hierarchies. Similarly, in Africa, the scramble for territories by European powers in the late 19th century disregarded existing ethnic and cultural boundaries, leading to conflicts that persist to this day.

Understanding the history of racism is crucial because it provides context for the systemic inequalities we see today. It shows us that racism is not just an individual failing but a deeply embedded system that has evolved over centuries. By examining this history, we can better understand the roots of contemporary racial issues and the ongoing struggle for equality and justice.

As we continue to explore this topic, it is important to recognize that history is not just a series of events but a complex web of causes and effects. The actions and ideologies of the past continue to shape our present and future. In the next pages, we will delve deeper into specific historical events and figures that have influenced the trajectory of racism, highlighting both the atrocities committed and the resistance movements that have fought against racial oppression.

As we delve further into the history of racism, it is essential to understand the pivotal role of colonialism in shaping racial attitudes and policies. The colonial era, spanning from the 15th to the 20th centuries, was a period marked by the expansion of European powers into Africa, Asia, and the Americas. This era was characterized by the establishment of colonies and the exploitation of indigenous populations, all justified through the lens of racial superiority.

The Spanish and Portuguese were among the first to embark on large-scale colonial enterprises. The conquest of the Americas, beginning with Christopher Columbus's voyages in 1492, led to the subjugation and near extermination of indigenous peoples. The encomienda system, where Spanish settlers were granted the right to extract labour and tribute from indigenous communities, epitomized the brutal exploitation justified by racial hierarchies. Indigenous peoples were viewed as inferior and in need of European "civilization," a notion that rationalized the violence and oppression they faced.

In the 17th century, British colonialism began to take shape, eventually becoming one of the most extensive empires in history. The British East India Company played a crucial role in the colonization of India, using both military force and political manipulation to establish control. British rule in India was marked by economic exploitation, cultural suppression, and the imposition of a racial hierarchy that privileged Europeans. The consequences of colonial policies, such as the partition of India in 1947, continue to affect the region's socio-political landscape.

Africa experienced some of the most severe impacts of European colonialism. The Berlin Conference of 1884-1885, also known as the Scramble for Africa, saw European powers divide the continent among themselves with little regard for existing ethnic and cultural boundaries. This arbitrary division laid the groundwork for many of the conflicts that plague Africa today. Colonization involved the extraction of resources and the exploitation of African labour, often through coercive systems such as forced labour and taxation.

In South Africa, British and Dutch colonization led to the institutionalization of racial segregation, culminating in the apartheid regime of the 20th century. Apartheid was a system of institutionalized racial segregation and discrimination that enforced the dominance of the white minority over the non-white majority. The resistance to apartheid, led by figures like Nelson Mandela and organizations such as the African National Congress, became a global symbol of the fight against racial oppression.

The Atlantic slave trade was another catastrophic consequence of colonial expansion. Beginning in the 15th century and continuing until the 19th century, millions of Africans were forcibly transported across the Atlantic to work as slaves in the Americas. This brutal system was driven by the demand for labour to cultivate lucrative cash crops like sugar, tobacco, and cotton. The dehumanization of African slaves was justified through pseudo-scientific racial theories that depicted them as inherently inferior and suited for enslavement.

In the United States, the legacy of slavery is deeply interwoven with the nation's history. The institution of slavery shaped the economic, social, and political foundations of the country. After the Civil War and the abolition of slavery in 1865, the Reconstruction era attempted to address the inequalities faced by formerly enslaved people. However, the end of Reconstruction led to the establishment of Jim Crow laws, which enforced racial segregation and disenfranchised Black Americans. The civil rights movement of the mid-20th century sought to dismantle these oppressive systems, leading to significant legislative changes, though many challenges remain.

The cultural impact of colonialism and slavery extended beyond laws and policies. Racist ideologies were propagated through literature, art, and science, reinforcing the notion of European superiority. The works of writers and thinkers like Rudyard Kipling, who famously referred to colonial subjects as "half-devil and half-child," exemplified the paternalistic and demeaning views that justified colonial rule. These cultural narratives helped to entrench racial hierarchies in the collective consciousness.

As we examine the history of racism, it is also important to recognize the resistance and resilience of oppressed peoples. From the Haitian Revolution, where enslaved Africans overthrew their French colonizers, to the independence movements across Africa and Asia, colonized peoples have continually fought for their freedom and dignity. These struggles have been instrumental in shaping the modern world and advancing the cause of racial justice.

Understanding the historical context of racism is crucial for comprehending its contemporary manifestations. The legacies of colonialism and slavery are still evident in the systemic inequalities and racial prejudices that persist today. By acknowledging and addressing this history, we can better understand the root causes of racism and work towards creating a more equitable and just society.

In the following pages, we will explore specific events and figures that have played a significant role in the history of racism. We will examine how these historical developments have influenced the present and consider the lessons they offer for the future. The journey through history is not just an academic exercise but a vital step in the ongoing struggle for racial equality and justice.

As we continue to explore the history of racism, it is important to highlight the role of pseudo-scientific theories in cementing racial hierarchies. During the 18th and 19th centuries, the rise of scientific racism provided a veneer of legitimacy to racist ideologies. These theories, often propagated by respected scientists and intellectuals, claimed to offer empirical evidence of the natural superiority of certain races over others.

One of the earliest and most influential proponents of scientific racism was Carl Linnaeus, a Swedish botanist who is best known for his work in classifying plants and animals. In his 1735 work Systema Naturae, Linnaeus also categorized humans into four distinct racial groups, assigning characteristics and behaviours to each. These classifications were not based on rigorous scientific evidence but rather on subjective observations and cultural biases.

Johann Friedrich Blumenbach, a German physician and anthropologist, further developed these ideas in the late 18th century. Blumenbach is often credited with coining the term "Caucasian" to describe people of European descent, whom he placed at the top of his racial hierarchy. His classification system divided humanity into five races: Caucasian, Mongolian, Malayan, Ethiopian, and American. Blumenbach's work, like that of Linnaeus, was based more on physical appearance and anecdotal evidence than on scientific rigor.

The 19th century saw the proliferation of these pseudo-scientific ideas, which were used to justify colonialism, slavery, and segregation. One of the most notorious examples of scientific racism is the work of Samuel Morton, an American physician who conducted studies on human skulls. Morton claimed that cranial capacity, or the volume of the skull, correlated with intelligence, and he used his measurements to argue that Europeans had the largest brains and were therefore the most intelligent race. Morton's methods were flawed and biased, but his conclusions were widely accepted and cited by proponents of racial hierarchy.

Another influential figure was Herbert Spencer, a British philosopher who applied Charles Darwin's theory of evolution to human societies. Spencer coined the term "survival of the fittest" and argued that social and economic inequalities were natural outcomes of the struggle for survival. This idea, known as Social Darwinism, provided a convenient justification for the exploitation and oppression of marginalized groups. It suggested that the success of European colonial powers and the wealth of the white upper class were evidence of their inherent superiority.

The impact of these pseudo-scientific theories extended beyond academia. They influenced public policy, legal systems, and social attitudes, reinforcing the belief in racial hierarchies. In the United States, for example, the notion of white superiority was enshrined in laws and practices that restricted the rights and opportunities of African Americans and other racial minorities. The eugenics movement, which gained prominence in the early 20th century, sought to improve the genetic quality of the human population by preventing those deemed "unfit" from reproducing. Eugenicists advocated for policies such as forced sterilization, which disproportionately targeted people of colour, the poor, and the disabled.

The horrors of Nazi Germany's racial policies during World War II, which were grounded in eugenic and pseudo-scientific theories of racial purity, brought about a significant shift in the global discourse on race. The atrocities committed by the Nazis, including the Holocaust, exposed the deadly consequences of scientific racism and led to a widespread rejection of these ideas. In the post-war period, the United Nations issued declarations affirming the equality of all human beings and condemning racial discrimination.

Despite these advances, the legacy of scientific racism continues to influence contemporary society. Implicit

biases and stereotypes rooted in these discredited
theories still persist, affecting how people perceive and
treat individuals of different races. Addressing these
biases requires ongoing education and a commitment to
promoting a more accurate and inclusive understanding
of human diversity.

As we examine the history of racism, it is essential to
recognize the resilience and resistance of those who have
been oppressed. Throughout history, marginalized
communities have fought against racist ideologies and
practices, often at great personal risk. Their efforts have
been instrumental in challenging and dismantling
systems of oppression.

One notable example is the abolitionist movement,
which emerged in the late 18th and early 19th centuries
to combat the institution of slavery. Abolitionists, both
Black and white, worked tirelessly to raise awareness
about the horrors of slavery and to advocate for its end.
Figures such as Frederick Douglass, Harriet Tubman,
and William Lloyd Garrison played crucial roles in this
struggle, using their voices and actions to challenge the
status quo and demand justice.

The civil rights movement of the mid-20th century is
another powerful testament to the strength and
determination of those who resist racism. Leaders like
Martin Luther King Jr., Rosa Parks, and Malcolm X
mobilized millions of people to demand equal rights and
an end to segregation and discrimination. Their efforts
led to significant legal and social changes, including the

Civil Rights Act of 1964 and the Voting Rights Act of 1965.

As we move forward, it is important to continue building on the legacy of these movements and to recognize that the fight against racism is ongoing. By understanding the historical roots of racism and the ways it has been challenged, we can better equip ourselves to address the systemic inequalities that persist today.

In the next pages, we will explore how racism has manifested in specific countries, examining the unique histories and contemporary challenges faced by different societies. By taking a global perspective, we can gain a more comprehensive understanding of the ways in which racism operates and the diverse strategies used to combat it.

As we turn our attention to specific countries, we begin with the United States, a nation whose history is profoundly shaped by the complexities of race and racism. The United States provides a poignant example of how racism can be deeply embedded in a nation's fabric, influencing its development and persisting into modern times.

The foundation of the United States was laid during an era when European settlers viewed the indigenous peoples of the Americas as inferior. This view justified the violent displacement and genocide of Native American populations, a dark chapter often glossed over in traditional narratives of American history. The

Doctrine of Discovery, endorsed by European monarchies and the Catholic Church, declared that lands not inhabited by Christians were available to be "discovered" and claimed. This doctrine provided a moral and legal justification for the colonization and exploitation of indigenous peoples.

The introduction of African slavery into the American colonies in the early 17th century marked another significant moment in the history of racism in the United States. The transatlantic slave trade forcibly brought millions of Africans to the Americas, where they were subjected to brutal conditions and denied basic human rights. Slavery became a cornerstone of the Southern economy, deeply entrenching racial hierarchies and fuelling economic growth through the exploitation of Black labour.

The abolition of slavery in 1865, following the Civil War, did not bring an end to racial discrimination. The Reconstruction era, a period of significant political and social upheaval, saw efforts to integrate formerly enslaved people into American society. Despite the initial promise of Reconstruction, including the passage of the 13th, 14th, and 15th Amendments, which aimed to grant citizenship and equal rights to Black Americans, the era ended with the resurgence of white supremacy and the establishment of Jim Crow laws.

Jim Crow laws enforced racial segregation and disenfranchised Black Americans, particularly in the Southern states. These laws, coupled with widespread acts of violence and intimidation, such as lynching, sought to maintain white dominance and prevent Black Americans from achieving social and economic parity. The legal and social systems were rigged to Favor whites, creating profound disparities in wealth, education, and political power that have long-lasting effects.

The civil rights movement of the 1950s and 1960s marked a critical turning point in the struggle against institutionalized racism in the United States. Led by figures such as Martin Luther King Jr., Rosa Parks, and Malcolm X, the movement employed tactics of nonviolent protest and civil disobedience to challenge segregation and demand equal rights. Landmark achievements, such as the Civil Rights Act of 1964 and the Voting Rights Act of 1965, were significant victories, yet the fight for racial equality continued.

Despite these legislative gains, systemic racism persisted. Issues such as redlining, mass incarceration, and economic inequality continued to disproportionately affect Black communities. The war on drugs, initiated in the 1980s, led to the over-policing and mass incarceration of African Americans, further entrenching racial disparities in the criminal justice system. Scholars like Michelle Alexander have argued that the criminal justice system functions as a "new Jim Crow," perpetuating a racial caste system that disenfranchises Black Americans.

The Black Lives Matter movement, which emerged in the 2010s, brought renewed attention to issues of police brutality and systemic racism. Sparked by the killings of unarmed Black individuals like Trayvon Martin, Michael Brown, and George Floyd, the movement mobilized millions of people worldwide to protest against racial injustice. It highlighted the enduring legacy of racism and the urgent need for reform in policing and other institutions.

The history of racism in the United States is a testament to the resilience and resistance of marginalized communities. Despite centuries of oppression, African Americans and other racial minorities have continually fought for their rights and dignity. Their struggles have shaped the nation's legal and cultural landscape, pushing the United States towards a more inclusive and equitable society.

Understanding this history is crucial for addressing the systemic inequalities that persist today. By recognizing the deep roots of racism and the ways it has been challenged, we can better understand the complexities of contemporary racial issues and work towards meaningful change.

In the next pages, we will explore the history of racism in other countries, each with its unique context and challenges. By examining these different perspectives, we can gain a more comprehensive understanding of the global nature of racism and the diverse strategies employed to combat it.

Turning our focus to the United Kingdom, we encounter a history of racism that is deeply intertwined with the legacy of the British Empire. The expansion of the British Empire from the 16th to the 20th centuries was driven by economic ambitions and the belief in the cultural and racial superiority of the British people. This belief justified the subjugation and exploitation of vast populations across Africa, Asia, and the Caribbean.

The British Empire's involvement in the transatlantic slave trade was a significant and grim chapter in its history. British ships transported millions of Africans to the Americas, where they were sold into slavery. The profits from the slave trade and the labour of enslaved people contributed significantly to the economic development of Britain. Cities like Liverpool and Bristol grew wealthy on the back of the slave trade, with many prominent families and institutions benefiting from this inhumane practice.

In the colonies, the British imposed racial hierarchies that privileged white settlers and administrators over the indigenous and enslaved populations. In India, for example, the British employed a policy of divide and rule, exacerbating ethnic and religious divisions to maintain control. British colonial rule in India led to significant economic exploitation, cultural suppression, and the implementation of a legal and social system that entrenched racial inequalities.

The end of World War II marked the beginning of the decolonization process, as countries in Africa, Asia, and the Caribbean fought for and gained independence. However, the legacy of colonialism left deep scars, with newly independent nations grappling with the economic and social challenges inherited from colonial rule. The process of decolonization also led to significant migration to the UK from former colonies, reshaping the demographic landscape and bringing issues of race and immigration to the forefront of British society.

Post-war Britain saw the arrival of the Windrush generation, named after the ship HMT Empire Windrush, which brought Caribbean migrants to the UK in 1948. These migrants were invited to help rebuild the country after the war, yet they faced significant racism and discrimination. They were often relegated to low-paying jobs, faced housing discrimination, and experienced hostility and violence from segments of the British population.

The racial tensions of the post-war period culminated in events like the 1958 Notting Hill riots, where white mobs attacked Caribbean immigrants, highlighting the deep-seated racial animosity. In response, the UK government introduced a series of immigration acts aimed at limiting the influx of non-white migrants, further entrenching racial divisions.

The civil rights movement in the United States inspired similar movements in the UK. Organizations like the Campaign Against Racial Discrimination (CARD) and later, the Black People's Day of Action, mobilized to fight against racial injustice and promote civil rights. The Race Relations Acts of 1965, 1968, and 1976 were significant legislative steps aimed at addressing racial discrimination and promoting equality. These acts made it illegal to discriminate on the grounds of race in public places, employment, and housing, and established the Commission for Racial Equality to enforce these laws.

Despite these legislative advances, racial inequality and discrimination persisted. Institutional racism, particularly within the police force, was brought to light by high-profile cases such as the murder of Stephen Lawrence in 1993. The subsequent Macpherson Report in 1999 concluded that the Metropolitan Police was institutionally racist, leading to widespread calls for reform.

The 21st century has seen ongoing efforts to address racial inequalities in the UK. Movements such as Black Lives Matter UK have highlighted issues of police brutality, racial profiling, and socio-economic disparities. The Windrush scandal, which emerged in the 2010s, exposed the wrongful detention and deportation of Caribbean migrants who had lived in the UK for decades, prompting a national outcry and demands for justice.

Understanding the history of racism in the UK is crucial for addressing contemporary racial issues. The legacy of colonialism, the impact of immigration policies, and the persistence of institutional racism are all factors that shape the experiences of racial minorities in Britain today. By acknowledging and addressing this history, we can work towards creating a more inclusive and equitable society.

In the following pages, we will explore the history of racism in other countries, examining how different historical contexts have shaped racial dynamics and the ongoing struggles for equality. By taking a global perspective, we can gain a deeper understanding of the universal and unique aspects of racism and the various ways in which it can be challenged.

Next, we turn our attention to South Africa, where the history of racism is indelibly marked by the system of apartheid. Apartheid, which means "apartness" in Afrikaans, was a policy of racial segregation and discrimination enforced by the National Party government from 1948 to 1994. This system institutionalized racial inequality and severely restricted the rights and freedoms of the non-white population.

The roots of apartheid can be traced back to earlier colonial policies implemented by the Dutch and British settlers. From the arrival of the Dutch East India Company in the 17th century, racial segregation was enforced through laws and practices that favoured white settlers over indigenous African populations and other racial groups. The British, who took control in the early 19th century, continued these policies, further entrenching racial divisions.

In the late 19th and early 20th centuries, as South Africa became an important hub for mining and agriculture, racial discrimination intensified. The discovery of diamonds and gold attracted significant European investment and led to the establishment of a complex labour system designed to exploit African workers. Laws such as the 1913 Natives Land Act restricted black South Africans from owning land, confining them to reserves and paving the way for large-scale land dispossession.

The formal establishment of apartheid in 1948 marked the beginning of an era of even more explicit and brutal racial segregation. The apartheid regime categorized the population into four racial groups: white, black, coloured (mixed race), and Indian. Each group was subjected to different laws and restrictions, with the white population enjoying the most privileges.

Under apartheid, non-white South Africans were forced to live in designated areas, often in overcrowded and under-resourced townships. The Group Areas Act of 1950 legalized the forced removal of non-white communities from areas designated for white occupation. Education, healthcare, and other public services were segregated, with vastly inferior provisions for the non-white population.

The apartheid government also imposed severe restrictions on movement and employment. The pass laws required black South Africans to carry identification documents at all times, controlling their movement and employment opportunities. Failure to produce a pass could result in arrest and imprisonment. These laws severely limited the economic and social mobility of the black population, creating a system of exploitation and control.

Resistance to apartheid was met with brutal repression. The African National Congress (ANC), founded in 1912, became the leading organization in the fight against apartheid. Figures such as Nelson Mandela, Oliver Tambo, and Walter Sisulu emerged as key leaders, advocating for nonviolent protest and civil disobedience. However, the Sharpeville Massacre of 1960, where police killed 69 unarmed protesters, marked a turning point, leading to increased militancy within the anti-apartheid movement.

The ANC and other resistance groups, such as the Pan Africanist Congress (PAC) and the South African Communist Party (SACP), were banned, and many of their leaders were imprisoned or forced into exile. Nelson Mandela's imprisonment in 1962 became a global symbol of the struggle against apartheid. Despite the harsh repression, the resistance continued, both within South Africa and internationally.

International solidarity and pressure played a crucial role in the fight against apartheid. The global anti-apartheid movement, supported by governments, organizations, and individuals worldwide, imposed economic sanctions and cultural boycotts on the apartheid regime. These measures, combined with internal resistance, gradually weakened the apartheid state.

The eventual dismantling of apartheid began in the late 1980s, culminating in the release of Nelson Mandela in 1990 and the subsequent negotiations that led to the first multiracial elections in 1994. The ANC, led by Mandela, won these elections, marking the end of apartheid and the beginning of a new era for South Africa.

The transition to democracy was marked by efforts to address the legacy of apartheid through reconciliation and justice. The Truth and Reconciliation Commission (TRC), chaired by Archbishop Desmond Tutu, was established to document human rights abuses committed during the apartheid era and to promote national healing. While the TRC played a crucial role in acknowledging the atrocities of the past, many challenges remain in addressing the deep-seated economic and social inequalities left by apartheid.

The history of racism in South Africa is a powerful reminder of the resilience and determination of oppressed peoples. The struggle against apartheid, with its global support and local activism, demonstrates the potential for solidarity and collective action to bring about profound social change. Today, South Africa continues to grapple with the legacies of apartheid, striving towards a more just and equitable society.

In the next chapter, we will examine the various forms of racism, from overt discrimination to subtle microaggressions. By understanding the different

manifestations of racism, we can better recognize and
address it in our efforts to create a more inclusive world.

Chapter 3: Racism in the USA

The United States offers a particularly vivid case study
of how racism can evolve and persist in different forms
throughout a nation's history. From the days of colonial
settlement to the modern era, racial discrimination has
been a constant, albeit changing, feature of American
society. This chapter will delve into the key events,
policies, and movements that have shaped racial
dynamics in the USA.

The origins of racism in the United States are closely tied
to the establishment of European colonies in the 17th
century. Early settlers brought with them beliefs in white
superiority and the right to dominate non-European
peoples. These attitudes were reinforced by economic
interests, particularly the desire for cheap labour to
support the burgeoning agricultural economy. The
introduction of African slavery in the early 1600s
marked a significant turning point, institutionalizing a
system of racial hierarchy that would persist for
centuries.

The transatlantic slave trade forcibly brought millions of
Africans to the American colonies, where they were
subjected to brutal conditions and denied basic human
rights. Slavery became a cornerstone of the Southern
economy, deeply entrenching racial hierarchies and

fuelling economic growth through the exploitation of Black labour. The legal and social systems of the colonies and, later, the United States were designed to maintain this racial order, with laws that codified the status of enslaved people and denied them any semblance of personhood.

The abolition of slavery in 1865, following the Civil War, was a significant milestone, but it did not bring an end to racial discrimination. The Reconstruction era, a period of significant political and social upheaval, saw efforts to integrate formerly enslaved people into American society. Despite the initial promise of Reconstruction, including the passage of the 13th, 14th, and 15th Amendments, which aimed to grant citizenship and equal rights to Black Americans, the era ended with the resurgence of white supremacy and the establishment of Jim Crow laws.

Jim Crow laws enforced racial segregation and disenfranchised Black Americans, particularly in the Southern states. These laws, coupled with widespread acts of violence and intimidation, such as lynching, sought to maintain white dominance and prevent Black Americans from achieving social and economic parity. The legal and social systems were rigged to favour whites, creating profound disparities in wealth, education, and political power that have long-lasting effects.

The Great Migration, which began in the early 20th century, saw millions of African Americans move from the rural South to urban areas in the North and West in search of better opportunities and to escape the oppressive conditions of the Jim Crow South. This migration led to significant demographic shifts and contributed to the growth of Black urban communities. However, it also exposed African Americans to new forms of racial discrimination in housing, employment, and education.

The civil rights movement of the 1950s and 1960s marked a critical turning point in the struggle against institutionalized racism in the United States. Led by figures such as Martin Luther King Jr., Rosa Parks, and Malcolm X, the movement employed tactics of nonviolent protest and civil disobedience to challenge segregation and demand equal rights. Landmark achievements, such as the Civil Rights Act of 1964 and the Voting Rights Act of 1965, were significant victories, yet the fight for racial equality continued.

Despite these legislative gains, systemic racism persisted. Issues such as redlining, mass incarceration, and economic inequality continued to disproportionately affect Black communities. The war on drugs, initiated in the 1980s, led to the over-policing and mass incarceration of African Americans, further entrenching racial disparities in the criminal justice system. Scholars like Michelle Alexander have argued that the criminal justice system functions as a "new Jim Crow," perpetuating a racial caste system that disenfranchises Black Americans.

The rise of the Black Lives Matter movement in the 2010s brought renewed attention to issues of police brutality and systemic racism. Sparked by the killings of unarmed Black individuals like Trayvon Martin, Michael Brown, and George Floyd, the movement mobilized millions of people worldwide to protest against racial injustice. It highlighted the enduring legacy of racism and the urgent need for reform in policing and other institutions.

Understanding the history of racism in the United States is crucial for addressing the systemic inequalities that persist today. The legacy of slavery, segregation, and discriminatory policies continues to shape the social, economic, and political landscape. By recognizing and addressing this history, we can work towards creating a more inclusive and equitable society.

In the following pages, we will explore specific events and figures that have played a significant role in the history of racism in the United States. We will examine how these historical developments have influenced the present and consider the lessons they offer for the future. The journey through history is not just an academic exercise but a vital step in the ongoing struggle for racial equality and justice.

As we delve deeper into the history of racism in the United States, it is essential to highlight key events and figures that have shaped the nation's racial landscape. These events not only reveal the persistent and evolving nature of racism but also underscore the resilience and resistance of marginalized communities.

One pivotal event was the Dred Scott decision of 1857. Dred Scott, an enslaved African American man, sued for his freedom on the grounds that he had lived in free territories. The U.S. Supreme Court, however, ruled that African Americans, whether free or enslaved, were not citizens and had no right to sue in federal court. This decision reinforced the idea of Black inferiority and highlighted the deep entrenchment of racism in American legal and political systems.

The Civil War, fought from 1861 to 1865, was primarily driven by the issue of slavery. The Union's victory led to the abolition of slavery with the 13th Amendment. However, the post-war Reconstruction era, which sought to rebuild the South and integrate formerly enslaved people into society, faced significant resistance. The rise of white supremacist groups like the Ku Klux Klan and the implementation of Black Codes aimed to restrict the newfound freedoms of African Americans and maintain white dominance.

The early 20th century witnessed the resurgence of the Ku Klux Klan and the implementation of Jim Crow laws, which legalized racial segregation in the Southern United States. Public facilities, schools, transportation, and even neighborhoods were segregated, and the principle of "separate but equal" established by the 1896 Plessy v. Ferguson Supreme Court decision ensured that these practices remained in place for decades. The reality, however, was that facilities for Black Americans were vastly inferior to those for whites, perpetuating systemic inequality.

During this period, the Great Migration saw millions of African Americans move to Northern and Western cities in search of better opportunities and to escape the oppressive conditions of the South. While this migration led to the growth of vibrant Black urban communities, such as Harlem in New York City, it also exposed African Americans to new forms of racial discrimination, including discriminatory housing practices like redlining.

Redlining, a practice where banks and insurers refused to offer loans or insurance to people living in certain neighborhoods based on racial composition, had profound long-term effects on Black communities. It contributed to the economic disenfranchisement of African Americans, limiting their ability to build wealth through homeownership and exacerbating economic disparities.

The civil rights movement of the 1950s and 1960s was a defining moment in the fight against racial injustice. Key events such as the Montgomery Bus Boycott, sparked by Rosa Parks' refusal to give up her seat to a white passenger, and the March on Washington, where Martin Luther King Jr. delivered his iconic "I Have a Dream" speech, galvanized national and international support for the cause. The movement's nonviolent protests and civil disobedience led to significant legislative achievements, including the Civil Rights Act of 1964 and the Voting Rights Act of 1965.

Despite these successes, the civil rights movement also faced fierce opposition. Activists were met with violent resistance, including police brutality, bombings, and assassinations. The death of leaders like Martin Luther King Jr. highlighted the high cost of the struggle for equality and underscored the deep-rooted nature of racism in American society.

In the decades following the civil rights movement, the fight against systemic racism continued. The 1980s and 1990s saw the rise of the war on drugs, which disproportionately targeted Black and Latino communities. Harsh sentencing laws and aggressive policing practices led to the mass incarceration of people of colour, creating a new form of racial control. Scholars like Michelle Alexander have argued that the criminal justice system functions as a "new Jim Crow," perpetuating racial inequality under the guise of crime control.

The 21st century has seen the emergence of the Black Lives Matter movement, which has brought renewed attention to issues of police brutality and systemic racism. The killings of unarmed Black individuals such as Trayvon Martin, Michael Brown, Eric Garner, and George Floyd sparked widespread protests and calls for accountability. The movement has highlighted the persistent racial disparities in policing and criminal justice, as well as broader issues of economic and social inequality.

Understanding the history of racism in the United States requires acknowledging both the progress made and the challenges that remain. The legacies of slavery, segregation, and discriminatory policies continue to shape the social, economic, and political landscape. By examining these historical events and figures, we can gain a deeper understanding of the systemic nature of racism and the ongoing struggle for equality.

In the following pages, we will explore the experiences of various racial and ethnic groups in the United States, examining how different communities have navigated and resisted racial discrimination. By taking a holistic view, we can better appreciate the complexity and diversity of the American experience and the continuous efforts to achieve justice and equality for all.

The experiences of different racial and ethnic groups in the United States highlight the multifaceted nature of racism and the diverse strategies of resistance employed by these communities. While African Americans have been the most visibly affected by systemic racism, other groups, including Native Americans, Asian Americans, and Latino Americans, have also faced significant discrimination and have their own unique histories of struggle and resilience.

Native Americans, the original inhabitants of the land, experienced devastating impacts from European colonization. The arrival of European settlers brought disease, warfare, and displacement, leading to dramatic population declines and the loss of traditional lands. The U.S. government pursued policies aimed at assimilating Native Americans into white society, often through coercive means such as the establishment of Indian boarding schools. These schools sought to eradicate indigenous cultures by prohibiting native languages and customs, causing deep psychological and cultural trauma.

The forced removal of Native Americans from their ancestral lands, exemplified by events such as the Trail of Tears, resulted in immense suffering and loss. The implementation of treaties that were often violated by the U.S. government further marginalized Native American communities. Despite these hardships, Native Americans have continuously fought to preserve their cultures and rights. The American Indian Movement (AIM), founded in the late 1960s, advocated for civil rights, sovereignty, and the protection of sacred lands, playing a crucial role in raising awareness and effecting change.

Asian Americans have also faced a history of exclusion and discrimination. The Chinese Exclusion Act of 1882 was the first significant law restricting immigration based on race, reflecting widespread anti-Chinese sentiment. Chinese immigrants, who came to the United States in large numbers during the Gold Rush and to work on the transcontinental railroad, were often met with hostility and violence. This law was followed by other exclusionary policies, such as the Immigration Act of 1924, which severely limited immigration from Asia.

During World War II, Japanese Americans were subjected to one of the most egregious violations of civil rights in U.S. history. Following the attack on Pearl Harbor, over 120,000 Japanese Americans, most of whom were U.S. citizens, were forcibly relocated to internment camps. This mass incarceration, based solely on race, was justified by unfounded fears of espionage and disloyalty. The internment left lasting scars on the Japanese American community, both economically and psychologically. It was not until 1988 that the U.S. government formally apologized and provided reparations to the surviving internees through the Civil Liberties Act.

Latino Americans, a diverse group encompassing people of Mexican, Puerto Rican, Cuban, Central American, and South American descent, have faced various forms of discrimination throughout U.S. history. The annexation of Texas and the Mexican American War in the mid-19th century resulted in the incorporation of large Mexican populations into the United States, often leading to their marginalization and disenfranchisement. Latino workers, particularly in agriculture, have historically been subject to exploitation and poor working conditions, a reality brought to light by the efforts of labour leaders like César Chávez and Dolores Huerta, who founded the United Farm Workers (UFW) union.

The civil rights struggle of Latino Americans have paralleled those of other racial and ethnic groups. The Chicano Movement of the 1960s and 1970s sought to address issues of educational inequality, political representation, and labour rights. Organizations like the National Council of La Raza (now UnidosUS) have played a significant role in advocating for the rights and advancement of Latino communities.

Each of these groups' experiences underscores the pervasive and systemic nature of racism in the United States. They also highlight the importance of intersectionality in understanding how different forms of oppression intersect and compound the challenges faced by individuals and communities. The intersection of race with factors such as immigration status, language, and cultural identity creates unique dynamics that must be addressed in efforts to promote racial justice.

In examining the history of racism in the United States, it is essential to recognize the contributions and resilience of these diverse communities. Their struggles and triumphs have shaped the nation's history and continue to influence contemporary movements for social justice. By understanding these histories, we can better appreciate the complexity of the American racial landscape and the ongoing efforts to achieve equality and inclusion.

In the next pages, we will delve into the specific experiences and contributions of these and other marginalized groups in the United States. By exploring their histories and contemporary challenges, we can gain a deeper understanding of the multifaceted nature of racism and the diverse strategies of resistance employed to combat it.

The experiences of Native Americans, African Americans, Asian Americans, and Latino Americans reveal the varied and complex ways racism manifests in the United States. To further understand the depth and breadth of this issue, it is essential to consider how these communities have contributed to American society, often in the face of immense adversity.

Native Americans, despite centuries of oppression and displacement, have maintained and revitalized their cultural heritage. Their contributions to environmental stewardship, art, and governance provide invaluable insights and enrich the broader American cultural tapestry. The sovereignty of Native American tribes, recognized through treaties and federal law, allows for a degree of self-governance that is critical for preserving cultural practices and addressing community-specific needs.

Environmental activism among Native Americans has been particularly impactful. The Standing Rock Sioux Tribe's resistance to the Dakota Access Pipeline in 2016 brought global attention to indigenous rights and environmental justice. This movement highlighted the ongoing struggle to protect sacred lands and resources from exploitation and underscored the intersection of environmental and racial justice.

African Americans have profoundly influenced American culture, politics, and society. From the Harlem Renaissance, which celebrated Black art, literature, and music in the 1920s, to the civil rights movement of the 1960s, African Americans have been at the forefront of social change. The contributions of African American artists, musicians, writers, and activists have shaped American identity and continue to inspire global movements for justice and equality.

In politics, figures like Shirley Chisholm, the first Black woman elected to the United States Congress, and Barack Obama, the first African American president, have broken significant barriers. Their achievements symbolize the ongoing struggle for representation and equity in American political life. The Black Lives Matter movement, founded in 2013, represents the latest chapter in this long history of activism, addressing systemic racism and advocating for justice for Black communities.

Asian Americans, a diverse group encompassing individuals of Chinese, Japanese, Korean, Filipino, Indian, Vietnamese, and many other descents, have also made significant contributions. The labour of Chinese immigrants was instrumental in building the transcontinental railroad, a vital infrastructure project that connected the country. Despite facing exclusionary laws and internment, Asian Americans have excelled in various fields, from science and technology to arts and culture.

The recent rise in anti-Asian hate crimes, exacerbated by the COVID-19 pandemic, has galvanized Asian American communities to advocate for their rights and safety. Organizations like Stop AAPI Hate have documented incidents of violence and discrimination, raising awareness and pushing for policy changes to protect Asian Americans.

Latino Americans, with their rich and varied heritage, have contributed immensely to the cultural, economic, and political life of the United States. From the influence of Mexican American culture in the Southwest to the contributions of Puerto Rican and Cuban communities in cities like New York and Miami, Latino culture is an integral part of the American mosaic. Latino workers are essential to various industries, including agriculture, construction, and hospitality, often performing vital yet undervalued labour.

The political influence of Latino Americans is also growing. Leaders like Alexandria Ocasio-Cortez and Julián Castro have emerged as prominent voices in national politics, advocating for issues such as immigration reform, healthcare, and economic justice. The increasing political mobilization of Latino communities reflects their rising demographic significance and their potential to shape the future of American politics.

In addition to these groups, other communities, such as Arab Americans, Jewish Americans, and LGBTQ+ individuals, face unique forms of discrimination that intersect with issues of race and ethnicity. The experiences of these groups further illustrate the complexity of racism in the United States and the importance of an intersectional approach to understanding and addressing these issues.

Arab Americans, for example, have faced increased scrutiny and discrimination, particularly after the events of September 11, 2001. Islamophobia and anti-Arab sentiment have led to profiling, hate crimes, and discriminatory policies. Organizations like the Arab American Institute work to advocate for the rights and representation of Arab Americans, highlighting the need for solidarity and support across communities.

Jewish Americans, who have contributed significantly to American culture, science, and politics, have also faced anti-Semitism. The resurgence of white nationalist movements and hate crimes targeting Jewish communities underscore the persistent threat of bigotry. Advocacy groups like the Anti-Defamation League (ADL) continue to fight against anti-Semitism and promote tolerance and inclusion.

The LGBTQ+ community, which includes individuals of all racial and ethnic backgrounds, faces unique challenges related to both sexual orientation and gender identity. The intersection of these identities with race can compound experiences of discrimination and marginalization. Advocacy for LGBTQ+ rights, led by organizations such as the Human Rights Campaign, emphasizes the need for inclusive policies that address the specific needs of LGBTQ+ individuals, particularly those from marginalized racial and ethnic groups.

Understanding the multifaceted nature of racism in the United States requires acknowledging the diverse experiences and contributions of these various communities. By recognizing and addressing the specific challenges faced by different groups, we can work towards a more inclusive and equitable society.

In the next pages, we will delve into the concept of institutional racism, exploring how systemic discrimination is embedded in the structures and institutions of American society. By examining the ways in which institutional racism operates, we can better understand the pervasive nature of racial inequality and identify strategies for dismantling these oppressive systems.

The experiences of Native Americans, African Americans, Asian Americans, and Latino Americans reveal the varied and complex ways racism manifests in the United States. To further understand the depth and breadth of this issue, it is essential to consider how these communities have contributed to American society, often in the face of immense adversity.

Native Americans, despite centuries of oppression and displacement, have maintained and revitalized their cultural heritage. Their contributions to environmental stewardship, art, and governance provide invaluable insights and enrich the broader American cultural tapestry. The sovereignty of Native American tribes, recognized through treaties and federal law, allows for a degree of self-governance that is critical for preserving cultural practices and addressing community-specific needs.

Environmental activism among Native Americans has been particularly impactful. The Standing Rock Sioux Tribe's resistance to the Dakota Access Pipeline in 2016 brought global attention to indigenous rights and environmental justice. This movement highlighted the ongoing struggle to protect sacred lands and resources from exploitation and underscored the intersection of environmental and racial justice.

African Americans have profoundly influenced American culture, politics, and society. From the Harlem Renaissance, which celebrated Black art, literature, and music in the 1920s, to the civil rights movement of the 1960s, African Americans have been at the forefront of social change. The contributions of African American artists, musicians, writers, and activists have shaped American identity and continue to inspire global movements for justice and equality.

In politics, figures like Shirley Chisholm, the first Black woman elected to the United States Congress, and Barack Obama, the first African American president, have broken significant barriers. Their achievements symbolize the ongoing struggle for representation and equity in American political life. The Black Lives Matter movement, founded in 2013, represents the latest chapter in this long history of activism, addressing systemic racism and advocating for justice for Black communities.

Asian Americans, a diverse group encompassing individuals of Chinese, Japanese, Korean, Filipino, Indian, Vietnamese, and many other descents, have also made significant contributions. The labour of Chinese immigrants was instrumental in building the transcontinental railroad, a vital infrastructure project that connected the country. Despite facing exclusionary laws and internment, Asian Americans have excelled in various fields, from science and technology to arts and culture.

The recent rise in anti-Asian hate crimes, exacerbated by the COVID-19 pandemic, has galvanized Asian American communities to advocate for their rights and safety. Organizations like Stop AAPI Hate have documented incidents of violence and discrimination, raising awareness and pushing for policy changes to protect Asian Americans.

Latino Americans, with their rich and varied heritage, have contributed immensely to the cultural, economic, and political life of the United States. From the influence of Mexican American culture in the Southwest to the contributions of Puerto Rican and Cuban communities in cities like New York and Miami, Latino culture is an integral part of the American mosaic. Latino workers are essential to various industries, including agriculture, construction, and hospitality, often performing vital yet undervalued labour.

The political influence of Latino Americans is also growing. Leaders like Alexandria Ocasio-Cortez and Julián Castro have emerged as prominent voices in national politics, advocating for issues such as immigration reform, healthcare, and economic justice. The increasing political mobilization of Latino communities reflects their rising demographic significance and their potential to shape the future of American politics.

In addition to these groups, other communities, such as Arab Americans, Jewish Americans, and LGBTQ+ individuals, face unique forms of discrimination that intersect with issues of race and ethnicity. The experiences of these groups further illustrate the complexity of racism in the United States and the importance of an intersectional approach to understanding and addressing these issues.

Arab Americans, for example, have faced increased scrutiny and discrimination, particularly after the events of September 11, 2001. Islamophobia and anti-Arab sentiment have led to profiling, hate crimes, and discriminatory policies. Organizations like the Arab American Institute work to advocate for the rights and representation of Arab Americans, highlighting the need for solidarity and support across communities.

Jewish Americans, who have contributed significantly to American culture, science, and politics, have also faced anti-Semitism. The resurgence of white nationalist movements and hate crimes targeting Jewish communities underscore the persistent threat of bigotry. Advocacy groups like the Anti-Defamation League (ADL) continue to fight against anti-Semitism and promote tolerance and inclusion.

The LGBTQ+ community, which includes individuals of all racial and ethnic backgrounds, faces unique challenges related to both sexual orientation and gender identity. The intersection of these identities with race can compound experiences of discrimination and marginalization. Advocacy for LGBTQ+ rights, led by organizations such as the Human Rights Campaign, emphasizes the need for inclusive policies that address the specific needs of LGBTQ+ individuals, particularly those from marginalized racial and ethnic groups.

Understanding the multifaceted nature of racism in the United States requires acknowledging the diverse experiences and contributions of these various communities. By recognizing and addressing the specific challenges faced by different groups, we can work towards a more inclusive and equitable society.

In the next pages, we will delve into the concept of institutional racism, exploring how systemic discrimination is embedded in the structures and institutions of American society. By examining the ways in which institutional racism operates, we can better understand the pervasive nature of racial inequality and identify strategies for dismantling these oppressive systems.

Institutional racism, also known as systemic racism, refers to the policies, practices, and norms entrenched within institutions that disproportionately disadvantage people of colour. This form of racism is pervasive and often subtle, making it particularly insidious and difficult to dismantle. By examining key institutions such as the criminal justice system, education, healthcare, and housing, we can gain a clearer understanding of how systemic racism operates and its profound impact on marginalized communities.

The criminal justice system is one of the most glaring examples of institutional racism in the United States. Disparities in arrest rates, sentencing, and incarceration highlight how people of colour, particularly African Americans and Latinos, are disproportionately targeted and punished. Studies have shown that Black individuals are more likely to be stopped by police, searched, and arrested compared to their white counterparts. Once arrested, they are also more likely to receive harsher sentences for similar crimes.

The war on drugs, initiated in the 1980s, exacerbated these disparities. Policies like mandatory minimum sentencing and the three-strikes law led to a surge in the incarceration of non-violent offenders, disproportionately affecting Black and Latino communities. The result has been the mass incarceration of people of colour, with devastating effects on families and communities. This system not only strips individuals of their freedom but also their ability to vote, secure employment, and reintegrate into society.

Education is another institution where systemic racism is deeply embedded. From funding disparities to discriminatory disciplinary practices, students of colour often face significant barriers to academic success. Schools in predominantly Black and Latino neighborhoods are frequently underfunded, lacking the resources and support necessary for student achievement. This funding gap contributes to the achievement gap, where students of colour lag behind their white peers in standardized test scores, graduation rates, and college enrolment.

Disciplinary practices also reflect racial biases. Black students, for instance, are more likely to be suspended or expelled for minor infractions compared to white students. These punitive measures contribute to the school-to-prison pipeline, where marginalized students are funnelled out of the educational system and into the criminal justice system. Addressing these issues requires comprehensive reforms to ensure equitable funding, culturally responsive teaching, and restorative justice practices in schools.

Healthcare disparities are another critical aspect of systemic racism. Racial and ethnic minorities often receive lower quality healthcare compared to white patients, leading to worse health outcomes. Factors such as implicit bias among healthcare providers, lack of access to care, and socio-economic barriers contribute to these disparities. For example, Black women are more likely to die from pregnancy-related complications than white women, regardless of income or education level.

The COVID-19 pandemic has further exposed these healthcare inequalities. Communities of colour have experienced higher rates of infection and mortality, underscoring the systemic factors that contribute to health disparities. These include limited access to healthcare, higher rates of pre-existing conditions, and socio-economic challenges that make it harder to adhere to public health guidelines. Addressing these disparities requires targeted interventions to improve access to care, reduce bias, and address the social determinants of health.

Housing policies have also played a significant role in perpetuating racial inequality. Historical practices like redlining and discriminatory lending have contributed to residential segregation and the racial wealth gap. Redlining, a practice where banks refused to offer loans in predominantly non-white neighborhoods, prevented many people of colour from buying homes and building wealth. This segregation has long-term effects, as neighborhoods with high concentrations of poverty and limited resources continue to struggle with underfunded schools, poor health outcomes, and increased crime rates.

Even today, people of colour face barriers in the housing market. Studies have shown that Black and Latino applicants are more likely to be denied mortgages and charged higher interest rates compared to white applicants with similar financial profiles. Additionally, zoning laws and gentrification can displace long-standing communities of colour, further entrenching economic disparities.

Addressing institutional racism requires a multi-faceted approach that includes policy reforms, education, and advocacy. It involves not only recognizing and dismantling discriminatory practices but also promoting equity and inclusion at all levels of society. Efforts to address systemic racism must be comprehensive and sustained, targeting the root causes of inequality and fostering an environment where all individuals have the opportunity to thrive.

In the next chapter, we will explore the concept of hidden racism, examining the subtle and often unconscious ways in which racial biases manifest in everyday interactions and societal norms. By understanding these covert forms of racism, we can better address the full spectrum of racial discrimination and work towards a more inclusive society.

Chapter 4: Racism in the UK

The United Kingdom has its own unique history of racism, influenced significantly by its colonial past and the waves of immigration that followed the decolonization process. Understanding racism in the UK requires an examination of both historical and contemporary contexts, including the legacy of the British Empire, the impact of immigration policies, and the ongoing challenges faced by ethnic minorities.

The British Empire, at its height, controlled vast territories across Africa, Asia, the Caribbean, and the Pacific. The justification for this imperial expansion was often rooted in racial superiority, with the belief that British rule was bringing "civilization" to the "uncivilized" parts of the world. This paternalistic attitude masked the exploitation, violence, and oppression that characterized colonial rule. Indigenous populations were subjected to brutal treatment, land dispossession, and cultural erasure.

The legacy of colonialism continues to influence racial dynamics in the UK. After World War II, Britain experienced significant immigration from its former colonies. The arrival of the Windrush generation in 1948 marked the beginning of large-scale immigration from the Caribbean, followed by waves of migrants from South Asia and Africa. These immigrants were invited to help rebuild the country after the war, but they faced significant racism and discrimination upon arrival.

In the post-war period, immigrants from the Commonwealth were often relegated to low-paying jobs and faced housing discrimination. The Notting Hill riots of 1958, where white mobs attacked Caribbean immigrants, highlighted the racial tensions of the time. These events led to the introduction of the Commonwealth Immigrants Act in 1962, which sought to restrict immigration from non-white Commonwealth countries. This act was the first in a series of immigration laws aimed at curbing the influx of non-white migrants.

The 1960s and 1970s saw the emergence of anti-racist movements in the UK, inspired by the civil rights struggles in the United States. Organizations like the Campaign Against Racial Discrimination (CARD) and the British Black Panthers mobilized to fight against racial injustice and promote civil rights. The Race Relations Acts of 1965, 1968, and 1976 were significant legislative steps aimed at addressing racial discrimination and promoting equality. These acts made it illegal to discriminate on the grounds of race in public places, employment, and housing, and established the Commission for Racial Equality to enforce these laws.

Despite these legislative advances, racial inequality and discrimination persisted. Institutional racism, particularly within the police force, was brought to light by high-profile cases such as the murder of Stephen Lawrence in 1993. The subsequent Macpherson Report in 1999 concluded that the Metropolitan Police was institutionally racist, leading to widespread calls for reform. The report's findings emphasized the need for greater accountability and transparency within law enforcement and other public institutions.

In the 21st century, the UK continues to grapple with issues of racism and immigration. The Windrush scandal, which emerged in the 2010s, exposed the wrongful detention and deportation of Caribbean migrants who had lived in the UK for decades. This scandal highlighted the hostile environment policies implemented by the government, which aimed to make life difficult for undocumented immigrants but also affected long-standing residents. The public outcry and demands for justice led to apologies and compensation for the affected individuals, but it also underscored the systemic nature of racial discrimination in immigration policies.

The rise of Islamophobia has also been a significant concern in recent years. Muslims in the UK face discrimination and hostility, often fuelled by media portrayals and political rhetoric that associate Islam with terrorism. Hate crimes against Muslims have increased, and there have been calls for greater protection and support for Muslim communities. The Prevent strategy, part of the government's counter-terrorism efforts, has been criticized for disproportionately targeting Muslims and fostering mistrust.

The Black Lives Matter movement has had a global impact, resonating strongly in the UK. Protests against police brutality and systemic racism have brought renewed attention to the experiences of Black Britons and other ethnic minorities. The toppling of the statue of Edward Colston, a prominent slave trader, during a protest in Bristol in 2020, sparked a nationwide debate about the legacy of colonialism and the representation of historical figures in public spaces.

Racial disparities in health, education, and employment continue to be significant issues. The COVID-19 pandemic has exacerbated these inequalities, with ethnic minorities experiencing higher rates of infection and mortality. This has prompted calls for a comprehensive approach to addressing health disparities and ensuring equitable access to healthcare.

Efforts to combat racism in the UK must address both the historical legacies and contemporary manifestations of racial inequality. This involves not only legal and policy reforms but also cultural and educational initiatives to promote understanding and inclusion. Schools, workplaces, and public institutions must take active steps to recognize and dismantle systemic racism, ensuring that all individuals, regardless of their background, have the opportunity to thrive.

In the next pages, we will delve deeper into specific events and figures that have shaped the history of racism in the UK, examining how these developments have influenced the present and what lessons they offer for the future. Understanding this history is crucial for addressing the systemic inequalities that persist and working towards a more just and inclusive society.
To gain a deeper understanding of the history of racism in the UK, it is essential to explore specific events and figures that have significantly influenced racial dynamics. These stories not only highlight the struggles faced by ethnic minorities but also the resilience and activism that have driven progress toward equality.

One of the earliest and most significant figures in the fight against racism in the UK was Olaudah Equiano. Born in what is now Nigeria, Equiano was enslaved as a child and transported to the Caribbean and later to England. After purchasing his freedom, he became a prominent abolitionist and author. His autobiography, The Interesting Narrative of the Life of Olaudah Equiano, published in 1789, provided a powerful firsthand account of the horrors of slavery and played a crucial role in the abolitionist movement. Equiano's eloquent writing and tireless campaigning helped to raise awareness and build support for the abolition of the transatlantic slave trade, which was eventually abolished in 1807.

The abolition of the slave trade did not end racial discrimination in the UK. Throughout the 19th and early 20th centuries, racial prejudices persisted, often exacerbated by the British Empire's colonial policies. The Empire Exhibition in 1924, held in Wembley, London, exemplified the era's attitudes. The exhibition showcased the achievements of the British Empire, but it also reinforced stereotypes and racial hierarchies by depicting colonized peoples as exotic and inferior.

The arrival of the Windrush generation in 1948 marked a new chapter in the UK's racial history. The Empire Windrush brought over 500 passengers from the Caribbean to the UK, invited to help rebuild the country after World War II. These immigrants and their descendants faced significant challenges, including racism, discrimination, and social exclusion. Despite these obstacles, they made substantial contributions to British society, particularly in sectors such as healthcare, transport, and industry.

One of the most significant events highlighting racial tensions in the post-war period was the Notting Hill riots of 1958. Tensions had been brewing in the multicultural neighborhood of Notting Hill, where many Caribbean immigrants had settled. Over several nights, white mobs attacked Black residents, resulting in violent clashes. The riots exposed the deep-seated racism within British society and led to calls for better protection and integration of immigrants.

The 1960s and 1970s saw the rise of organized anti-racist activism. The Campaign Against Racial Discrimination (CARD), founded in 1964, aimed to combat racial inequality through political lobbying and public education. The British Black Panthers, inspired by their American counterparts, were established in 1968 and focused on addressing police brutality and advocating for civil rights. Leaders such as Darcus Howe and Althea Jones-LeCointe played pivotal roles in these movements, raising awareness and pushing for legislative changes.

The murder of Stephen Lawrence in 1993 was a watershed moment in the UK's struggle against racism. Stephen, an 18-year-old Black student, was brutally attacked and killed by a gang of white youths in a racially motivated crime. The initial police investigation was marred by incompetence and racial bias, leading to widespread public outcry. The subsequent Macpherson Inquiry concluded that the Metropolitan Police was institutionally racist, prompting significant reforms within the police force and other public institutions.

The Windrush scandal of the 2010s brought to light the systemic failures in the UK's immigration policies. Long-term Caribbean residents, who had lived in the UK legally for decades, were wrongly detained, denied legal rights, and threatened with deportation. The scandal highlighted the hostile environment policy's devastating impact, leading to apologies from the government and compensation for the affected individuals. It also underscored the need for a more humane and just immigration system.

In recent years, the Black Lives Matter movement has had a profound impact in the UK. The death of George Floyd in the United States in 2020 sparked global protests, including significant demonstrations across Britain. The movement has brought renewed attention to issues of police brutality, systemic racism, and the legacy of colonialism. The toppling of the Edward Colston statue in Bristol during a Black Lives Matter protest symbolized the broader reckoning with Britain's colonial past and its present-day implications.

Efforts to address racism in the UK have also included educational and cultural initiatives. The decolonization of the curriculum in schools and universities aims to provide a more inclusive and accurate representation of history. Initiatives like Black History Month, celebrated every October in the UK, seek to highlight the contributions of Black individuals to British society and to educate the public about the ongoing struggle for racial equality.

Despite these efforts, significant challenges remain. Racial disparities in health, education, employment, and the criminal justice system continue to affect ethnic minorities. The COVID-19 pandemic has highlighted these inequalities, with higher infection and mortality rates among Black and Asian communities. Addressing these issues requires sustained commitment and comprehensive strategies that involve policy reforms, community engagement, and a commitment to equity and inclusion.

Understanding the history of racism in the UK is crucial for creating a more just and inclusive society. By acknowledging past injustices and recognizing the contributions and resilience of ethnic minorities, we can work towards dismantling systemic racism and promoting equality for all.

In the next pages, we will explore the experiences of specific ethnic groups in the UK, examining how they have navigated and resisted racial discrimination. By taking a closer look at these communities, we can gain a deeper understanding of the diverse and multifaceted nature of racism in Britain.

To fully understand the complexities of racism in the UK, it is important to examine the experiences of specific ethnic groups, including Black Britons, South Asians, and Eastern Europeans. Each of these groups has faced unique challenges and has contributed to the rich tapestry of British society in distinct ways.

 Black Britons

The Black British community has a long and varied history, beginning with the presence of Black individuals in Britain dating back to Roman times. However, the most significant waves of immigration occurred in the post-war period, particularly with the arrival of the Windrush generation. These Caribbean immigrants and their descendants have made significant contributions to British culture, society, and economy, despite facing persistent racism and discrimination.

The Black community in the UK has been at the forefront of the struggle for racial equality. The 1981 Brixton riots, sparked by tensions between Black youth and the police, were a turning point in race relations. These riots highlighted the systemic discrimination faced by Black Britons, including disproportionate stop-and-search practices and police brutality. The subsequent Scarman Report acknowledged the existence of institutional racism and called for reforms within the police force.

Cultural contributions from the Black British community have also been significant. The Notting Hill Carnival, originally started by Trinidadian Claudia Jones in 1959, has grown into one of the largest street festivals in

Europe, celebrating Caribbean culture and heritage. In the arts, figures like Zadie Smith in literature, Steve McQueen in film, and Stormzy in music have achieved international acclaim, showcasing the diversity and talent within the Black British community.

 South Asians

The South Asian community in the UK, comprising individuals of Indian, Pakistani, Bangladeshi, and Sri Lankan descent, has a significant presence, particularly in cities like London, Birmingham, and Leicester. Many South Asians arrived in the UK during the mid-20th century, initially as part of the labour force needed to rebuild the country after World War II. Subsequent waves of immigration included those fleeing conflict and persecution, such as the Ugandan Asians expelled by Idi Amin in the 1970s.

South Asians in the UK have faced various forms of discrimination, including violence, as exemplified by the 1976 Southall riots, where tensions between the local Asian community and far-right groups culminated in violent clashes. Despite these challenges, the South Asian community has made substantial contributions to British society, particularly in business, healthcare, and education.

Culturally, South Asians have enriched the UK with their traditions, cuisine, and festivals. The celebration of Diwali and Eid has become an integral part of the British multicultural landscape. In the arts, authors like Salman

Rushdie and Monica Ali, musicians like Nitin Sawhney, and actors like Dev Patel have made significant impacts, highlighting the contributions of South Asians to British culture.

Eastern Europeans

The enlargement of the European Union in 2004 led to significant immigration from Eastern European countries such as Poland, Lithuania, and Romania. Eastern European immigrants have contributed to various sectors, including construction, agriculture, and healthcare. However, they have also faced hostility and discrimination, often fuelled by political rhetoric and media portrayals that depict them as a burden on the welfare system or as taking jobs from British citizens.

The Brexit referendum in 2016 exacerbated tensions, with reports of increased hate crimes against Eastern Europeans. The uncertainty surrounding their legal status post-Brexit has further marginalized these communities. Despite these challenges, Eastern Europeans have shown resilience, building vibrant communities and contributing to the cultural and economic fabric of the UK.

Intersectionality and Solidarity

The experiences of these ethnic groups illustrate the multifaceted nature of racism in the UK. Intersectionality, a concept introduced by Kimberlé Crenshaw, helps us understand how different forms of discrimination intersect and compound the challenges faced by individuals. For example, a Black woman might experience racism and sexism simultaneously, affecting her opportunities and treatment in society.

Solidarity among different ethnic and racial groups is crucial in the fight against racism. By recognizing the commonalities in their struggles, communities can work together to advocate for equity and justice. The Black Lives Matter protests in the UK saw support from a diverse array of groups, demonstrating the power of collective action.

Education plays a vital role in fostering understanding and combating racism. Schools and universities must ensure that the curriculum reflects the diversity of British society and includes the histories and contributions of all ethnic groups. Initiatives like decolonizing the curriculum aim to provide a more inclusive and accurate representation of history, challenging the Eurocentric narratives that have long dominated education.

Media representation is another critical area for addressing racism. Positive and accurate portrayals of ethnic minorities can help challenge stereotypes and promote understanding. The success of shows like Michaela Coel's, I May Destroy You and Riz Ahmed's Mogul Mowgli underscores the importance of diverse voices in media and the arts.

Moving Forward

Addressing racism in the UK requires a comprehensive and sustained effort involving policy reforms, education, and cultural change. It involves listening to the voices of marginalized communities and taking concrete actions to dismantle systemic barriers. By recognizing the contributions and struggles of all ethnic groups, the UK can move towards a more inclusive and equitable society.

In the next chapter, we will explore the concept of slavery and its enduring impact on racial relations. By examining the history of slavery and its legacy, we can better understand the deep roots of racial inequality and the ongoing efforts to achieve justice and reparations.

The influence of colonialism, immigration, and the persistent efforts of ethnic minorities to secure their rights form the bedrock of understanding racism in the UK. As we delve deeper into the individual stories and systemic issues, we uncover the complex and multifaceted nature of racial discrimination that persists today.

The Role of Colonial Legacy

The British Empire's colonial past has left an indelible mark on contemporary British society. The economic exploitation and cultural dominance exercised over colonies established a racial hierarchy that persists in subtle and overt ways. This legacy is visible in the socioeconomic disparities and the representation of ethnic minorities in various sectors.

For instance, the education system in Britain has long been criticized for its Eurocentric curriculum that often marginalizes the contributions and histories of non-European peoples. Efforts to decolonize the curriculum aim to rectify this by incorporating diverse perspectives and highlighting the impacts of colonialism. Such initiatives are crucial for fostering a more inclusive and accurate understanding of history among students.

Institutional Racism in Modern Britain

Institutional racism in the UK manifests in various sectors, including policing, healthcare, and employment. The Macpherson Report's identification of institutional racism within the Metropolitan Police was a landmark moment, prompting reforms and increased scrutiny of police practices. However, issues such as racial profiling and disproportionate use of force against ethnic minorities remain significant concerns.

In healthcare, the disparities are stark. Black and Asian individuals often receive lower quality care and face barriers to accessing healthcare services. The higher mortality rates from COVID-19 among these communities underscore the urgent need for systemic change in healthcare delivery and policies to ensure equitable treatment.

Employment discrimination continues to be a significant barrier for ethnic minorities. Studies have shown that candidates with ethnic-sounding names are less likely to be called for interviews compared to their white counterparts with identical qualifications. This bias extends to promotions and career advancement, contributing to the racial pay gap and limiting economic opportunities for ethnic minorities.

 Cultural Contributions and Resistance

Despite the challenges, ethnic minorities have made profound contributions to British culture, enriching it with diverse traditions, art, and perspectives. The influence of Caribbean, South Asian, African, and other cultures is evident in British music, literature, cuisine, and fashion.

The arts have been a powerful medium for resistance and expression. Artists, writers, and musicians from ethnic minority backgrounds have used their platforms to challenge stereotypes, highlight injustices, and celebrate their heritage. The success of British-Nigerian author Bernardine Evaristo, who won the Booker Prize for her novel Girl, Woman, Other, and the critical acclaim for the film Lovers Rock by Steve McQueen, are testaments to the vibrancy and impact of minority voices in British culture.

Grassroots movements and community organizations play a crucial role in advocating for the rights of ethnic minorities. Groups such as the Runnymede Trust and the Joint Council for the Welfare of Immigrants work tirelessly to address issues of racial inequality, immigration, and social justice. These organizations provide vital support, conduct research, and lobby for policy changes to create a more equitable society.

The Future of Race Relations in the UK

Addressing racism in the UK requires a multifaceted approach that includes policy reforms, education, and community engagement. Legal protections against discrimination must be robustly enforced, and institutions need to be held accountable for their practices. Diversity and inclusion initiatives should not be superficial but must aim to create genuine opportunities for underrepresented groups.

Education is a critical tool for combating racism. Schools and universities must commit to providing an inclusive curriculum that reflects the diverse history and contributions of all ethnic groups. This involves training teachers to handle discussions on race sensitively and effectively, ensuring that all students feel valued and understood.

Public awareness campaigns and media representation are also vital in challenging stereotypes and promoting understanding. Positive and accurate portrayals of ethnic minorities in media can help shift public perceptions and reduce prejudice. Supporting minority-owned businesses and initiatives can also foster economic empowerment and community resilience.

The history and ongoing challenges of racism in the UK highlight the need for continued vigilance and action.

While progress has been made, significant work remains to address the systemic inequalities that persist. By acknowledging the contributions and struggles of ethnic minorities and committing to sustained efforts for change, the UK can move towards a more inclusive and just society.

In the next chapter, we will explore the concept of slavery and its enduring impact on racial relations. By examining the history of slavery and its legacy, we can better understand the deep roots of racial inequality and the ongoing efforts to achieve justice and reparations.

Chapter 5: Racism in Other Countries

Racism is a global phenomenon, manifesting in various forms and intensities across different regions and cultures. By examining the experiences of racism in countries such as Australia, South Africa, India, and Brazil, we can gain a broader understanding of how racial discrimination operates and the unique challenges faced by different communities. This chapter delves into the historical contexts and contemporary realities of racism in these countries, highlighting both the struggles and the progress made in combating racial inequality.

Australia

Australia's history of racism is deeply intertwined with its colonial past and the treatment of its Indigenous peoples. The arrival of British settlers in 1788 marked the beginning of a brutal campaign against the Aboriginal and Torres Strait Islander peoples. The doctrine of terra nullius, meaning "land belonging to no one," was used to justify the dispossession of Indigenous lands and the denial of their rights.

The colonization process involved widespread violence, forced relocations, and the introduction of diseases that decimated Indigenous populations. Policies such as the forced removal of Indigenous children from their families, known as the Stolen Generations, aimed to assimilate Indigenous peoples into white society and erase their cultural identities. These children were often placed in institutions or with non-Indigenous families, where they were subjected to abuse and neglect.

The impact of these policies continues to affect Indigenous communities today. Indigenous Australians face significant disparities in health, education, employment, and housing compared to the non-Indigenous population. Efforts to address these inequalities include land rights movements, which have sought to reclaim traditional lands, and the establishment of organizations like the Aboriginal Legal Service, which provides legal assistance to Indigenous peoples.

In recent years, there has been a growing recognition of the need for reconciliation and justice. The 2008 apology by then-Prime Minister Kevin Rudd to the Stolen Generations was a significant step towards acknowledging past wrongs. However, ongoing issues such as the high rates of Indigenous incarceration and deaths in custody highlight the continued struggle for equality and justice.

 South Africa

South Africa's history of racism is dominated by the apartheid era, a system of institutionalized racial segregation and discrimination that lasted from 1948 to 1994. Apartheid, meaning "apartness" in Afrikaans, was designed to maintain white minority rule over the country's Black majority and other racial groups, including Coloureds and Indians.

Under apartheid, South Africans were classified by race, and these classifications determined every aspect of their lives, including where they could live, work, and go to school. Black South Africans were forcibly removed from their homes and relocated to underdeveloped and overcrowded townships. They were denied basic rights and subjected to harsh laws designed to suppress dissent.

The resistance to apartheid was met with brutal repression. Leaders like Nelson Mandela, Oliver Tambo, and Walter Sisulu were imprisoned, and anti-apartheid organizations like the African National Congress (ANC) were banned. Despite this, the struggle for freedom continued, both within South Africa and internationally.

The end of apartheid in 1994, marked by the election of Nelson Mandela as the country's first Black president, was a significant victory for racial justice. The establishment of the Truth and Reconciliation Commission (TRC), chaired by Archbishop Desmond Tutu, aimed to address the human rights abuses of the apartheid era and promote national healing. The TRC provided a platform for victims and perpetrators to share their stories and seek forgiveness.

Despite these efforts, South Africa continues to face significant challenges. Economic disparities remain stark, with the Black majority still experiencing high levels of poverty and unemployment. Efforts to address these inequalities include land reform programs and affirmative action policies aimed at redressing the imbalances created by apartheid.

India

In India, racism often intersects with caste discrimination, creating a complex web of social hierarchies. The caste system, a traditional Hindu social stratification, categorizes individuals into rigid groups based on their birth. While the Indian Constitution abolished untouchability and prohibits caste-based discrimination, the legacy of the caste system continues to influence social dynamics and contribute to inequality.

Dalits, formerly known as "untouchables," face significant discrimination and violence. They are often denied access to basic resources, education, and employment opportunities. Efforts to address caste discrimination include affirmative action policies, such as reservations in education and government jobs for Scheduled Castes and Scheduled Tribes.

In addition to caste, racial discrimination in India also affects individuals from the northeastern states and African immigrants. People from the northeastern region, who often have distinct physical features, face prejudice and are subjected to derogatory stereotypes. African immigrants, particularly students, have reported incidents of violence and discrimination, reflecting the broader issues of xenophobia and racism in Indian society.

Activism and advocacy play a crucial role in combating these forms of discrimination. Organizations like the National Campaign on Dalit Human Rights (NCDHR) work to raise awareness and promote the rights of marginalized communities. Legal reforms and public education campaigns are also essential in challenging deep-seated prejudices and promoting social inclusion.

Brazil

Brazil, often celebrated for its racial and cultural diversity, has a complex history of racism rooted in its colonial past and the legacy of slavery. Brazil was the last country in the Americas to abolish slavery in 1888, and the effects of this history are still evident today. Afro-Brazilians, who make up a significant portion of the population, continue to face systemic racism and economic disparities.

Racial discrimination in Brazil is often manifested in subtle ways, through social and economic exclusion. Afro-Brazilians are disproportionately represented in low-income neighborhoods, have lower levels of education, and face barriers to employment and healthcare. Police violence against Black Brazilians is also a significant issue, with frequent reports of extrajudicial killings and abuses.

Efforts to address racial inequality in Brazil include affirmative action policies in education and employment, aimed at increasing opportunities for Afro-Brazilians. Cultural movements, such as the Black Consciousness Movement, have also played a vital role in promoting racial pride and challenging discriminatory practices.

In recent years, there has been a growing recognition of the need to address Brazil's racial inequalities. Activists and organizations continue to push for comprehensive reforms and greater representation of Afro-Brazilians in all sectors of society.

The global nature of racism highlights the interconnected struggles of marginalized communities across different countries. While the specific manifestations of racism may vary, the underlying issues of inequality and discrimination are universal. Understanding the historical and contemporary contexts of racism in countries like Australia, South Africa, India, and Brazil provides valuable insights into the broader fight for racial justice.

By learning from these diverse experiences, we can develop more effective strategies to combat racism and promote equality worldwide. In the next chapter, we will explore the enduring impact of slavery and its legacy on racial relations, examining how the history of slavery continues to shape contemporary issues of racial inequality and justice.

To understand the enduring impact of slavery on racial relations, it is essential to explore the history of slavery and its legacy. Slavery, particularly the transatlantic slave trade, is one of the most brutal and inhumane practices in human history, with long-lasting effects that continue to shape contemporary societies. This chapter delves into the history of slavery, its abolition, and the ongoing struggle for justice and reparations.

The Transatlantic Slave Trade

The transatlantic slave trade, which spanned from the 15th to the 19th centuries, forcibly transported millions of Africans to the Americas. This trade was driven by the demand for labour to cultivate cash crops such as sugar, tobacco, and cotton. The brutal conditions aboard slave ships, where enslaved Africans were chained and packed tightly, led to high mortality rates. Those who survived the journey faced a life of forced labour, violence, and dehumanization.

The economic benefits of the slave trade were immense for European colonial powers and their American colonies. The wealth generated from slave labour contributed significantly to the development of Western economies, funding industrialization and expanding global trade networks. However, this economic gain came at an enormous human cost, with entire African societies disrupted and millions of lives lost or forever altered.

Slavery in the Americas

In the Americas, slavery became the foundation of the colonial economy, particularly in the Southern United States, the Caribbean, and Brazil. Enslaved Africans were forced to work on plantations under harsh conditions, with little regard for their well-being. The legal system codified the status of enslaved people as property, stripping them of their rights and humanity.

The resistance of enslaved people was a constant threat to the institution of slavery. From daily acts of defiance to organized rebellions, enslaved Africans continually fought for their freedom. Notable uprisings, such as the Haitian Revolution, where enslaved Africans successfully overthrew French colonial rule, demonstrated the resilience and agency of those oppressed by slavery.

Abolition and Its Aftermath

The abolition of slavery was a protracted and contentious process, marked by the efforts of abolitionists and the resistance of those who benefited from the institution. In the United Kingdom, the abolitionist movement gained momentum in the late 18th century, with figures like

William Wilberforce advocating for the end of the transatlantic slave trade. The trade was abolished in 1807, followed by the emancipation of enslaved people in British colonies in 1833.

In the United States, the abolition of slavery was achieved through the Civil War (1861-1865). The Emancipation Proclamation in 1863 and the 13th Amendment in 1865 legally ended slavery, but the legacy of the institution continued to affect African Americans. The Reconstruction era (1865-1877) attempted to integrate formerly enslaved people into society, but the rise of Jim Crow laws and racial segregation perpetuated racial inequalities.

In Brazil, slavery persisted until 1888, making it the last country in the Americas to abolish the practice. The abolition did not result in significant social or economic improvements for Afro-Brazilians, who continued to face discrimination and marginalization.

The Legacy of Slavery

The legacy of slavery is evident in the systemic racial inequalities that persist in societies that practiced the transatlantic slave trade. The economic disparities, social exclusion, and racial prejudices rooted in slavery continue to affect descendants of enslaved people.

In the United States, the legacy of slavery is visible in the racial wealth gap, mass incarceration, and disparities in education, healthcare, and housing. The civil rights movement of the mid-20th century made significant strides in challenging segregation and discrimination, but the fight for racial justice continues.

Reparations for slavery have been a contentious issue. Advocates argue that reparations are necessary to address the historical injustices and ongoing inequalities faced by descendants of enslaved people. Proposals for reparations include financial compensation, educational scholarships, and policy reforms aimed at addressing systemic racism. Critics of reparations often cite practical and political challenges, but the debate continues as part of broader discussions about racial justice and reconciliation.

In the Caribbean, countries like Jamaica and Barbados have called for reparations from former colonial powers, arguing that the economic exploitation and social disruption caused by slavery have had lasting effects on their development. The CARICOM Reparations Commission, established by the Caribbean Community (CARICOM), advocates for reparatory justice, including debt cancellation, technology transfer, and the establishment of cultural institutions.

Contemporary Struggles and Movements

The fight against the legacy of slavery continues through various movements and initiatives. In the United States, the Black Lives Matter movement has brought renewed attention to issues of police brutality, systemic racism, and the need for comprehensive reforms. The movement has sparked global protests and discussions about racial justice, highlighting the enduring impact of slavery and the importance of addressing historical and contemporary injustices.

Education and public awareness are critical in understanding the full impact of slavery. Efforts to include the history of slavery and its legacy in school curricula aim to provide a more comprehensive understanding of racial dynamics and the roots of systemic inequality. Museums, memorials, and cultural institutions dedicated to preserving the history of slavery play a vital role in educating the public and honouring the memories of those who suffered under the institution.

The history of slavery and its legacy continue to shape contemporary racial relations. Understanding this history is crucial for addressing the systemic inequalities that persist and for promoting justice and reconciliation. By acknowledging the profound impact of slavery and supporting efforts for reparations and educational initiatives, societies can move towards a more equitable future.

In the next chapter, we will explore the various forms of racism, from overt discrimination to subtle microaggressions. By understanding these different manifestations, we can better recognize and address racism in our efforts to create a more inclusive world.

To further our understanding of the lasting impact of slavery, it is crucial to examine the various forms of racism that persist in society today. Racism manifests in numerous ways, from overt acts of discrimination to subtle, often unintentional, microaggressions. By exploring these different forms, we can better recognize and address the pervasive nature of racism.

Overt Racism

Overt racism is the most visible and explicit form of racial discrimination. It includes blatant acts of prejudice and discrimination, such as hate speech, racial slurs, and physical violence. Overt racism is often rooted in the belief in the superiority of one race over another and can manifest in both individual actions and institutional policies.

Hate crimes are a glaring example of overt racism. These crimes, motivated by racial hatred, can range from verbal harassment to physical assault and even murder. High-profile cases, such as the 2015 Charleston church shooting in the United States, where nine African American churchgoers were killed by a white supremacist, highlight the extreme violence that overt racism can entail.

In addition to individual acts, overt racism can be institutionalized through discriminatory laws and policies. For instance, apartheid in South Africa was a system of overt racial segregation and discrimination enforced by law. Similarly, the Jim Crow laws in the United States legally enforced racial segregation and disenfranchised Black Americans for decades.

Covert Racism

Covert racism, also known as hidden or subtle racism, is less visible but equally damaging. It involves discriminatory practices and attitudes that are not openly acknowledged or recognized. Covert racism can be intentional or unintentional and often operates through implicit biases and stereotypes.

Implicit bias refers to the unconscious attitudes and beliefs that individuals hold about different racial groups. These biases can influence behaviour and decision-making, often leading to discriminatory outcomes even when individuals are not consciously aware of their prejudices. For example, studies have shown that job applicants with ethnic-sounding names are less likely to be called for interviews compared to those with white-sounding names, even when their qualifications are identical.

Microaggressions are another form of covert racism. These are everyday verbal, nonverbal, and environmental slights or insults that communicate hostile or negative messages to people based on their race. Microaggressions can be subtle and may seem harmless to the perpetrator, but they can have a cumulative and damaging impact on the recipient. Examples of microaggressions include a person of colour being repeatedly asked, "Where are you really from?" or being told, "You're so articulate" in a tone that implies surprise.

Systemic Racism

Systemic racism, also known as institutional or structural racism, refers to the policies and practices embedded within institutions that produce and perpetuate racial inequalities. This form of racism is deeply ingrained in the fabric of society and affects multiple aspects of life, including education, employment, healthcare, and housing.

Systemic racism in education can be seen in the disparities in funding and resources available to schools serving predominantly minority communities. These schools often have fewer resources, less experienced teachers, and lower academic outcomes compared to schools in wealthier, predominantly white areas. This educational inequality contributes to the achievement gap and limits the opportunities available to students of colour.

In the healthcare system, systemic racism manifests in the disparities in access to care and health outcomes for different racial groups. Minority patients often receive lower quality care and face barriers to accessing healthcare services. For example, Black women in the United States are more likely to die from pregnancy-related complications than white women, a disparity that persists regardless of income or education level.

The criminal justice system is another area where systemic racism is prevalent. Racial disparities in arrest rates, sentencing, and incarceration highlight the unequal treatment of people of colour. The over-policing of minority communities and the disproportionate impact of the war on drugs on Black and Latino individuals are stark examples of systemic racism in action.

Cultural Racism

Cultural racism refers to the societal beliefs and practices that promote the idea that the culture and values of one racial group are superior to those of another. This form of racism is perpetuated through media representations, cultural norms, and institutional practices that marginalize and devalue the contributions and identities of minority groups.

Media representations play a significant role in shaping societal attitudes and perceptions. Stereotypical portrayals of racial and ethnic minorities in movies, television shows, and news reports can reinforce harmful stereotypes and contribute to the marginalization of these groups. For instance, the portrayal of Black individuals as criminals or Latinos as illegal immigrants perpetuates negative stereotypes that influence public perception and policy.

Cultural appropriation is another aspect of cultural racism. It involves the adoption or exploitation of elements of a minority culture by members of a dominant culture without understanding or respecting the original context. This can include the use of traditional clothing, hairstyles, music, and other cultural expressions in ways that trivialize their significance.

Addressing and Combating Racism

Addressing the various forms of racism requires a multifaceted approach that includes education, policy reforms, and community engagement. It involves recognizing and challenging our own biases, advocating for systemic changes, and promoting a culture of inclusion and respect.

Education is a powerful tool for combating racism. Schools and universities must provide curricula that reflect the diversity of experiences and contributions of all racial and ethnic groups. This includes teaching about the history of racism, the impact of slavery and colonialism, and the ongoing struggles for justice and equality.

Policy reforms are essential for addressing systemic racism. This includes implementing policies that promote equity in education, healthcare, employment, and housing. Legal protections against discrimination must be robustly enforced, and institutions must be held accountable for practices that perpetuate racial inequalities.

Community engagement and grassroots activism play a crucial role in driving social change. Organizations and movements that advocate for racial justice, such as Black Lives Matter, the NAACP, and other civil rights groups, are vital in raising awareness, mobilizing communities, and pushing for policy changes.

Understanding the various forms of racism is essential for effectively addressing and combating it. By recognizing the ways in which racism manifests, from overt discrimination to subtle microaggressions and systemic inequalities, we can develop more comprehensive strategies to promote equity and inclusion. The fight against racism requires collective effort, commitment, and a willingness to confront uncomfortable truths in order to create a more just and inclusive world.

In the next chapter, we will delve into the concept of institutional racism, exploring how systemic discrimination is embedded in the structures and institutions of society. By examining the ways in which institutional racism operates, we can better understand the pervasive nature of racial inequality and identify strategies for dismantling these oppressive systems.

Chapter 6: Slavery and Racism

Slavery represents one of the most brutal and dehumanizing forms of racism, leaving a legacy that continues to affect societies worldwide. This chapter delves into the history of slavery, its abolition, and the ongoing impact it has on racial relations and social structures. By examining these elements, we gain a deeper understanding of how the echoes of slavery continue to shape contemporary issues of racial inequality and justice.

The Origins and Expansion of Slavery

Slavery has existed in various forms throughout human history, but the transatlantic slave trade stands out due to its scale and impact. Beginning in the 15th century, European powers such as Portugal, Spain, Britain, France, and the Netherlands established vast networks for the capture, transport, and exploitation of African slaves. This trade was driven by the economic demand for labour to cultivate sugar, tobacco, cotton, and other cash crops in the Americas.

The process of capturing and transporting slaves was unimaginably brutal. Africans were kidnapped or bought from local rulers and forcibly marched to the coast, where they were held in squalid conditions before being shipped across the Atlantic. The Middle Passage, the sea journey from Africa to the Americas, was marked by extreme overcrowding, malnutrition, disease, and abuse. It is estimated that up to two million Africans died during this journey alone.

Upon arrival in the Americas, enslaved Africans were sold at auctions and forced to work on plantations, mines, and in households under harsh and often inhumane conditions. They were denied basic human rights, subjected to physical and psychological abuse, and regarded as property rather than people. The legal systems in slave-holding societies enshrined the status of slaves as chattel, perpetuating their exploitation and dehumanization.

The Economics of Slavery

The transatlantic slave trade and the institution of slavery were integral to the economic development of Europe and the Americas. The labour of enslaved Africans generated immense wealth for slave owners and colonial powers. The profits from plantations and other enterprises fuelled the growth of industries, cities, and trade networks in Europe.

In the United States, slavery became the economic backbone of the Southern states. The production of cotton, in particular, relied heavily on slave labour and became a cornerstone of the American economy. The wealth generated by slavery helped finance the industrialization of the Northern states, creating a complex economic interdependence between the North and the South.

The economic benefits of slavery extended beyond individual slave owners. Financial institutions, insurance companies, and businesses profited from the trade and exploitation of slaves. The legacy of this economic system is evident in the wealth disparities and economic structures that persist today.

Abolition Movements and the End of Slavery

The abolition of slavery was a protracted and contentious process. Abolitionist movements emerged in the late 18th and early 19th centuries, driven by moral, religious, and economic arguments against the institution. Prominent abolitionists such as William Wilberforce in Britain, Frederick Douglass in the United States, and Toussaint L'Ouverture in Haiti played crucial roles in advocating for the end of slavery.

In Britain, the abolitionist movement gained significant momentum in the late 18th century. The efforts of activists, combined with the testimonies of former slaves like Olaudah Equiano, raised public awareness and built support for abolition. The British Parliament passed the Abolition of the Slave Trade Act in 1807, which outlawed the transatlantic slave trade, and the Slavery Abolition Act in 1833, which ended slavery in British colonies.

In the United States, the abolition of slavery was achieved through the Civil War. The Emancipation Proclamation of 1863, issued by President Abraham Lincoln, declared the freedom of all enslaved people in Confederate-held territory. The passage of the 13th Amendment in 1865 formally abolished slavery throughout the United States. However, the end of slavery did not bring an end to racial discrimination and inequality.

Haiti's path to abolition was unique and remarkable. The Haitian Revolution, led by enslaved Africans and free people of colour, resulted in the overthrow of French colonial rule and the establishment of Haiti as the first independent Black republic in 1804. This revolution was both a significant blow to the institution of slavery and an inspiration for abolitionist movements worldwide.

The Legacy of Slavery

The legacy of slavery continues to shape racial relations and social structures in the contemporary world. The economic, social, and psychological impacts of slavery have created enduring inequalities and injustices that affect descendants of enslaved people.

Economic disparities are one of the most visible legacies of slavery. The wealth generated by slave labour was concentrated in the hands of slave owners and their descendants, while formerly enslaved people and their descendants were systematically excluded from economic opportunities. This has contributed to the significant racial wealth gap that persists today, particularly in countries like the United States and Brazil.

Socially, the dehumanisation and marginalization of enslaved people have left deep scars. Racial stereotypes and prejudices rooted in the institution of slavery continue to influence societal attitudes and behaviours. The systemic racism that developed during the era of slavery has evolved but remains embedded in institutions and policies, perpetuating inequality and discrimination.

Psychologically, the trauma of slavery has had lasting effects on descendants of enslaved people. The experience of being treated as property, subjected to violence, and denied basic human dignity has had intergenerational impacts on mental health and social well-being. Efforts to address these psychological scars include promoting cultural pride, resilience, and healing within affected communities.

 Reparations and Reconciliation

Reparations for slavery are a crucial aspect of addressing its legacy. Reparations involve compensating descendants of enslaved people for the injustices and economic exploitation their ancestors endured. Proposals for reparations include financial compensation, educational opportunities, policy reforms, and public acknowledgements of historical wrongs.

The debate over reparations is ongoing and contentious. Advocates argue that reparations are necessary to address the historical and ongoing inequalities faced by descendants of enslaved people. Critics often cite practical and political challenges, but the discussion remains vital to broader efforts to achieve racial justice and reconciliation.

In addition to reparations, efforts to promote reconciliation and healing are essential. Truth and reconciliation commissions, public apologies, and educational initiatives are critical in acknowledging past wrongs and fostering a collective commitment to addressing their legacy. These efforts aim to build a more inclusive and equitable society by recognizing the profound impact of slavery and supporting the descendants of those who suffered under its brutal regime.

The history of slavery and its legacy continue to shape contemporary racial relations and systemic inequalities. Understanding this history is crucial for addressing the ongoing impact of slavery and promoting justice and reconciliation. By acknowledging the profound effects of slavery and supporting efforts for reparations and healing, societies can move towards a more equitable and inclusive future.

In the next pages, we will explore the various forms of racism, from overt discrimination to subtle microaggressions. By understanding these different manifestations, we can better recognize and address racism in our efforts to create a more inclusive world.

To further understand the enduring impact of slavery, it is essential to explore the various ways in which the legacy of slavery has been addressed—or ignored—by different societies. This examination includes looking at the ongoing struggle for justice, the fight for reparations, and the broader efforts to reconcile with this dark chapter of history.

The Struggle for Justice and Equality

The abolition of slavery did not end the systemic inequalities faced by formerly enslaved people and their descendants. In many societies, the structures of racial discrimination that were built during the era of slavery evolved into new forms of oppression. Segregation, disenfranchisement, and economic exploitation continued to marginalize Black communities long after the formal end of slavery.

In the United States, the period following the Civil War, known as Reconstruction, was a time of significant progress and profound setbacks. Initially, Reconstruction brought about major advances, including the establishment of the Freedmen's Bureau, which assisted formerly enslaved people, and the passage of the 14th and 15th Amendments, which granted citizenship and voting rights. However, the end of Reconstruction in 1877 led to the rise of Jim Crow laws, which enforced racial segregation and disenfranchised Black Americans.

The civil rights movement of the mid-20th century was a pivotal response to these injustices. Leaders like Martin Luther King Jr., Malcolm X, Rosa Parks, and many others fought tirelessly for the dismantling of segregation and the recognition of Black Americans' civil rights. The movement achieved significant victories, including the Civil Rights Act of 1964 and the Voting Rights Act of 1965, but the struggle for racial equality continues.

The Fight for Reparations

Reparations for slavery remain a contentious and unresolved issue in many societies. The idea of reparations is rooted in the acknowledgement that the economic benefits derived from slavery have created lasting disparities that need to be addressed. Reparations seek to provide compensation and support to the descendants of enslaved people to help rectify these historical injustices.

In the United States, the push for reparations has gained renewed momentum in recent years. The aforementioned H.R. 40 bill, if passed, would create a commission to study and develop reparation proposals. This initiative reflects a growing recognition of the need to address the enduring impacts of slavery on Black Americans.

Reparations are not solely about financial compensation. They can also include initiatives such as educational scholarships, community investment programs, and efforts to preserve and celebrate Black culture and history. The goal is to create opportunities for economic empowerment and social upliftment for communities that have been historically marginalized.

Internationally, the call for reparations has also been significant. In the Caribbean, countries affected by slavery have formed the CARICOM Reparations Commission to seek reparations from former colonial powers. This movement highlights the global dimensions of the struggle for justice and the recognition of the lasting impacts of slavery.

Reconciliation and Healing

Reconciliation involves acknowledging the historical wrongs of slavery and working towards healing the wounds inflicted by this brutal institution. Truth and reconciliation commissions, public apologies, and educational initiatives are essential components of this process.

Truth and reconciliation commissions, such as those established in South Africa after the end of apartheid, provide a platform for victims and perpetrators to share their experiences and seek forgiveness. These commissions aim to promote healing and understanding by confronting the past and acknowledging the pain and suffering caused by systemic injustice.

Public apologies from governments and institutions that benefited from slavery are also important steps towards reconciliation. These apologies recognize the historical wrongs and the lasting impact of slavery, and they can help to foster a sense of justice and closure for affected communities.

Educational initiatives play a crucial role in reconciliation by ensuring that the history of slavery and its legacy is accurately and comprehensively taught. By educating future generations about the realities of slavery and the ongoing struggle for justice, societies can promote a more inclusive and equitable understanding of history.

The Global Legacy of Slavery

The legacy of slavery is not confined to the countries that practised it most extensively; it has had a global impact. The economic and social structures created by slavery have influenced international relations, trade, and cultural exchanges. The racial hierarchies established during the era of slavery have left a lasting imprint on global attitudes towards race and ethnicity.

In Latin America, the legacy of slavery is evident in the racial and economic disparities that persist in countries such as Brazil and Colombia. Afro-Latinx communities often face significant barriers to social and economic mobility, and efforts to address these inequalities are ongoing.

In Africa, the impact of the transatlantic slave trade is still felt in the form of disrupted societies and economies. The trade had a devastating effect on many African communities, stripping them of millions of their people and weakening social and economic structures. Efforts to address the legacy of slavery in Africa include initiatives to promote economic development and cultural revival.

The legacy of slavery also extends to the cultural and artistic contributions of the African diaspora. From music and dance to literature and visual arts, the cultural expressions of descendants of enslaved people have had a profound influence on global culture. These contributions are a testament to the resilience and creativity of Black communities in the face of historical and ongoing oppression.

Moving Forward

Addressing the legacy of slavery requires a multifaceted approach that includes reparations, reconciliation, and education. It involves a commitment to recognizing and rectifying the injustices of the past and promoting a more equitable future for all.

Reparations are a crucial component of this effort, providing a means to address the economic and social disparities created by slavery. Reconciliation initiatives, including truth and reconciliation commissions and public apologies, help to foster healing and understanding. Educational efforts ensure that the history and impact of slavery are accurately and comprehensively taught, promoting a more inclusive understanding of history.

By addressing the legacy of slavery, societies can move towards greater justice and equality. This process requires a collective commitment to confronting uncomfortable truths and working towards a more inclusive and equitable future.

In the next chapter, we will explore the various forms of racism, from overt discrimination to subtle microaggressions. By understanding these different manifestations, we can better recognize and address racism in our efforts to create a more inclusive world.

As we delve deeper into the lasting impacts of slavery, it is crucial to explore the different ways societies are working to address and rectify these historical injustices. This examination includes understanding how cultural memory, public policy, and grassroots movements play roles in shaping a more equitable future.

Cultural Memory and Public Acknowledgment

Cultural memory plays a significant role in how societies understand and process the legacy of slavery. Public acknowledgement of historical injustices is a critical step towards reconciliation. This involves not only formal apologies from governments and institutions but also the creation of memorials, museums, and educational programs that keep the memory of these events alive.

Memorials and museums dedicated to slavery provide spaces for reflection and education. The National Memorial for Peace and Justice in Montgomery, Alabama, for instance, commemorates the victims of racial terror lynchings and highlights the connection between slavery, segregation, and contemporary racial injustice. This memorial serves as a powerful reminder of the past and a call to action for the future.

In addition to physical memorials, cultural productions such as films, books, and art play a crucial role in shaping public memory. Works like the film 12 Years a Slave or the novel Beloved by Toni Morrison offer powerful narratives that bring the history of slavery into contemporary discourse. These cultural artefacts help to educate the public and foster empathy and understanding.

 Public Policy and Legislative Efforts

Addressing the legacy of slavery through public policy involves creating and implementing laws and programs that aim to reduce racial disparities and promote social justice. This includes policies aimed at economic empowerment, educational equity, healthcare access, and criminal justice reform.

Economic policies that promote wealth-building opportunities for descendants of enslaved people are essential. These can include initiatives such as grants for Black-owned businesses, housing subsidies, and tax incentives aimed at reducing the racial wealth gap. Such policies help to address the economic disadvantages that have been passed down through generations.

Educational equity is another critical area for public policy. Ensuring that all students have access to quality education, regardless of their racial or economic background, is vital for creating a more equitable society. This includes equitable funding for schools, affirmative action programs, and efforts to decolonize the curriculum to include a more comprehensive and inclusive portrayal of history.

Healthcare policies must also address the disparities faced by racial minorities. This involves improving access to quality healthcare, addressing implicit biases within the healthcare system, and ensuring that minority communities are adequately represented in medical research and healthcare decision-making processes.

Criminal justice reform is essential for addressing the legacy of slavery and systemic racism. This includes ending discriminatory policing practices, reforming sentencing laws that disproportionately affect Black and Latino communities and investing in community-based alternatives to incarceration. Efforts to restore voting rights to formerly incarcerated individuals and to address the criminalization of poverty are also crucial components of this reform.

Grassroots Movements and Activism

Grassroots movements and community activism play a vital role in pushing for social change and holding institutions accountable. These movements often emerge from the communities most affected by racial injustice and provide a platform for marginalized voices to be heard.

The Black Lives Matter movement, which began in 2013, has been instrumental in bringing attention to police brutality and systemic racism. Through protests, advocacy, and public education, Black Lives Matter has mobilized millions of people worldwide to demand justice and accountability. The movement has also highlighted the importance of intersectionality, recognizing that the fight for racial justice must also address issues of gender, sexuality, and economic inequality.

Community-based organizations are also crucial in providing support and resources to those affected by the legacy of slavery. These organizations often work at the grassroots level to address immediate needs such as housing, education, and healthcare while also advocating for broader systemic change. Groups like the NAACP, the Southern Poverty Law Centre, and the National Urban League have long histories of fighting for civil rights and social justice.

Healing and Reconciliation

Healing and reconciliation require both collective and individual efforts. At the collective level, truth and reconciliation commissions, public dialogues, and restorative justice programs can help to address historical and contemporary injustices. These initiatives provide spaces for truth-telling, accountability, and healing, fostering a sense of justice and closure.

At the individual level, healing involves recognizing and addressing the psychological impacts of slavery and racism. This includes providing mental health support and creating spaces where individuals can share their experiences and find solidarity and support. Efforts to promote cultural pride and resilience within Black communities are also vital components of this healing process.

The Role of International Solidarity

The struggle for racial justice is a global one, and international solidarity is essential for addressing the legacy of slavery. Collaborative efforts between countries, international organizations, and grassroots movements can help amplify the call for justice and promote shared strategies for combating racism.

International organizations such as the United Nations have recognized the need to address the legacy of slavery and have called for global action to combat racism and promote human rights. The UN's International Decade for People of African Descent (2015-2024) aims to recognize the contributions of people of African descent and promote their rights and inclusion worldwide.

Cross-cultural exchanges and partnerships between countries can also foster understanding and solidarity. These exchanges provide opportunities to learn from different experiences and to build a global movement for racial justice.

The legacy of slavery continues to shape contemporary racial relations and systemic inequalities. Addressing this legacy requires a multifaceted approach that includes cultural memory, public policy, grassroots activism, and international solidarity. By recognizing the profound impact of slavery and supporting efforts for justice and reconciliation, societies can move towards a more equitable and inclusive future.

In the next chapter, we will explore the various forms of racism, from overt discrimination to subtle microaggressions. By understanding these different manifestations, we can better recognize and address racism in our efforts to create a more inclusive world.

Exploring the nuances of how slavery has impacted societies and the various ways in which communities are addressing this legacy is crucial for understanding the pervasive nature of racism. In this section, we will delve deeper into specific case studies that highlight the efforts made towards justice and reconciliation in different regions, illustrating both successes and ongoing challenges.

Case Study: The United States

The United States, with its history deeply rooted in slavery and racial discrimination, offers a complex landscape of efforts towards justice and reconciliation. The civil rights movement of the 1950s and 1960s marked significant progress, but the country continues to grapple with the legacy of slavery and systemic racism.

One of the key initiatives in addressing this legacy has been the establishment of the Equal Justice Initiative (EJI) by Bryan Stevenson. EJI focuses on criminal justice reform, racial justice, and public education. The National Memorial for Peace and Justice, also known as the Lynching Memorial, was opened by EJI in 2018 in Montgomery, Alabama. This memorial is dedicated to the victims of lynching and aims to acknowledge the terror and violence inflicted on Black communities as part of America's history of racial injustice.

EJI's work extends beyond memorials to active legal advocacy, fighting for the rights of marginalized individuals and addressing wrongful convictions. Their efforts highlight the importance of both remembrance and direct action in the pursuit of justice.

Another significant development is the growing movement for reparations. Cities like Asheville, North Carolina, and Providence, Rhode Island, have begun to implement local reparations programs. These initiatives focus on addressing racial disparities in housing, education, and economic opportunities. By creating specific funds and programs, these cities are taking steps to acknowledge and rectify historical injustices.

Case Study: South Africa

South Africa's transition from apartheid to democracy is one of the most prominent examples of a country grappling with its legacy of institutionalized racial discrimination. The Truth and Reconciliation Commission (TRC), established in 1995 and chaired by Archbishop Desmond Tutu, played a pivotal role in addressing the atrocities committed during apartheid.

The TRC provided a platform for victims of human rights violations to share their stories and seek justice. It also allowed perpetrators of violence to come forward and request amnesty in exchange for full disclosure of their actions. The process aimed to promote healing and reconciliation by fostering a national dialogue about the past.

While the TRC was instrumental in acknowledging the pain and suffering caused by apartheid, South Africa continues to face significant challenges. Economic disparities remain stark, with Black South Africans still experiencing high levels of poverty and unemployment. Efforts to address these inequalities include affirmative action policies and land reform initiatives, but progress has been slow and contentious.

Case Study: Germany

Germany's approach to addressing the legacy of the Holocaust offers valuable lessons in dealing with historical injustices. The country has made significant efforts to atone for the atrocities committed during World War II and to educate future generations about the dangers of racism and xenophobia.

Germany's approach includes comprehensive education about the Holocaust in schools, public memorials such as the Holocaust Memorial in Berlin, and reparations to Holocaust survivors. The government's commitment to "never forget" serves as a powerful reminder of the importance of confronting the past to prevent future atrocities.

The German model emphasizes the importance of public acknowledgement, education, and reparations in addressing historical injustices. By facing its history head-on, Germany has taken steps to foster a culture of remembrance and responsibility.

 Case Study: Canada

Canada's efforts to address the legacy of residential schools and the broader treatment of Indigenous peoples highlight the ongoing struggle for reconciliation. The Truth and Reconciliation Commission of Canada, established in 2008, documented the history and lasting impacts of the residential school system, which forcibly removed Indigenous children from their families to assimilate them into Euro-Canadian culture.

The Commission's final report, released in 2015, included 94 Calls to Action aimed at redressing the legacy of residential schools and advancing the process of reconciliation. These recommendations encompass a wide range of areas, including education, health, justice, and language revitalization.

The Canadian government's response has included formal apologies, financial compensation to survivors, and efforts to implement the Calls to Action. However, significant work remains to address the systemic inequalities faced by Indigenous communities, including high rates of poverty, health disparities, and overrepresentation in the criminal justice system.

 The Importance of Education and Advocacy

Across these case studies, a common thread is the critical role of education and advocacy in addressing the legacy of slavery and systemic racism. Public education initiatives that include comprehensive histories of slavery and racism are essential for fostering a deeper understanding of these issues.

Advocacy groups and grassroots movements are also vital in pushing for policy changes and holding institutions accountable. These organizations often lead the charge in raising awareness, mobilizing communities, and advocating for justice and equality.

Efforts to include diverse voices and perspectives in these processes are crucial. Ensuring that the narratives and experiences of marginalized communities are heard and respected helps to create more inclusive and effective solutions.

Addressing the legacy of slavery and systemic racism requires a comprehensive approach that encompasses education, advocacy, policy reform, and community engagement. This section delves deeper into the strategies and initiatives that have been effective in various contexts, highlighting the importance of a multifaceted response to these enduring issues.

Educational Initiatives

Education is a cornerstone of efforts to address the legacy of slavery and promote racial justice. Comprehensive educational programs that include accurate histories of slavery and its impact are essential for fostering understanding and empathy.

Curriculum Reform: One of the most effective ways to address the legacy of slavery is through curriculum reform. Schools and universities must ensure that their curricula include detailed and accurate accounts of the history of slavery, colonialism, and their long-lasting impacts. This involves integrating the voices and experiences of marginalized communities into educational materials, providing students with a more inclusive and holistic understanding of history.

Cultural Competence Training: In addition to reforming curricula, educational institutions should implement cultural competence training for educators. This training helps teachers understand and address their own biases and equips them with the tools to create inclusive and supportive learning environments. By fostering cultural competence, educators can better support students from diverse backgrounds and promote an understanding of systemic racism.

Public Awareness Campaigns: Public awareness campaigns play a crucial role in educating the broader community about the history and legacy of slavery. These campaigns can include documentaries, public lectures, art exhibitions, and social media initiatives that highlight the experiences of enslaved people and their descendants. By raising awareness and fostering public dialogue, these initiatives can help to build a more informed and empathetic society.

Policy Reforms

Policy reforms are essential for addressing the systemic inequalities that stem from the legacy of slavery. These reforms must be comprehensive and targeted at dismantling the structures that perpetuate racial disparities.

Economic Empowerment: Economic policies aimed at reducing the racial wealth gap are crucial. This can include initiatives such as reparations, grants for minority-owned businesses, affordable housing programs, and workforce development initiatives. By providing economic opportunities and support, these policies can help to address the economic disadvantages created by centuries of exploitation and discrimination.

Healthcare Equity: Ensuring equitable access to healthcare is another critical area for policy reform. This involves addressing the social determinants of health, such as housing, education, and employment, that contribute to health disparities. Policies that promote diversity in the healthcare workforce, reduce implicit biases in medical treatment, and improve access to quality care for marginalized communities are essential for achieving health equity.

Criminal Justice Reform: The criminal justice system must be reformed to address the disproportionate impact of policing and incarceration on Black and Latino communities. This includes ending discriminatory policing practices, reforming sentencing laws, and investing in community-based alternatives to incarceration. Efforts to restore voting rights to formerly incarcerated individuals and to address the criminalization of poverty are also crucial components of this reform.

 Community Engagement and Grassroots Activism

Community engagement and grassroots activism are vital for driving social change and holding institutions accountable. These movements often emerge from the communities most affected by racial injustice and provide a platform for marginalized voices to be heard.

Grassroots Organizations: Grassroots organizations play a crucial role in advocating for racial justice and supporting marginalized communities. These organizations often work at the local level to address immediate needs such as housing, education, and healthcare while also advocating for broader systemic change. Groups like the NAACP, the Southern Poverty Law Centre, and the National Urban League have long histories of fighting for civil rights and social justice.

Community-Led Initiatives: Community-led initiatives, such as mutual aid networks and community development programs, are essential for building resilience and empowerment within marginalized communities. These initiatives often focus on addressing specific local issues and providing direct support to community members. By fostering solidarity and collective action, community-led initiatives can create lasting change from the ground up.

Youth Engagement: Engaging young people in the fight for racial justice is crucial for ensuring the sustainability of these efforts. Youth-led movements and organizations bring energy, creativity, and new perspectives to the struggle for equality. Programs that provide leadership training, mentorship, and opportunities for civic engagement can help to empower the next generation of activists and leaders.

Healing and Reconciliation

Healing and reconciliation are essential components of addressing the legacy of slavery and systemic racism. This involves both collective and individual efforts to acknowledge past wrongs, seek justice, and promote healing.

Truth and Reconciliation Commissions: Truth and reconciliation commissions provide a platform for victims and perpetrators of historical injustices to share their experiences and seek justice. These commissions aim to promote healing and understanding by fostering a national dialogue about the past and acknowledging the pain and suffering caused by systemic injustice. By confronting the truth, societies can begin the process of healing and reconciliation.

Restorative Justice Programs: Restorative justice programs focus on repairing the harm caused by racial injustice and promoting healing for both individuals and communities. These programs often involve facilitated dialogues between victims and offenders, community service, and other reparative actions. Restorative justice emphasizes accountability, empathy, and the importance of rebuilding relationships and trust.

Mental Health Support: Providing mental health support for individuals affected by the legacy of slavery and systemic racism is crucial for promoting healing. This includes access to culturally competent mental health services, support groups, and community-based healing practices. By addressing the psychological impacts of racial trauma, these services can help individuals and communities to heal and thrive.

The Role of International Solidarity

The struggle for racial justice is a global one, and international solidarity is essential for addressing the legacy of slavery. Collaborative efforts between countries, international organizations, and grassroots movements can help amplify the call for justice and promote shared strategies for combating racism.

International Collaboration: International organizations, such as the United Nations and the African Union, play a critical role in promoting racial justice and addressing the legacy of slavery. These organizations can facilitate dialogue, provide resources, and support efforts to combat racism and promote human rights worldwide.

Global Movements: Global movements for racial justice, such as the Black Lives Matter movement, demonstrate the power of international solidarity. These movements bring together activists from different countries to share experiences, strategies, and support. By building a global network of advocates, these movements can amplify their impact and drive meaningful change.

Cross-Cultural Exchanges: Cross-cultural exchanges and partnerships between countries can foster understanding and solidarity. These exchanges provide opportunities to learn from different experiences and to build a global movement for racial justice. Programs that facilitate cultural exchanges, international conferences, and collaborative projects can help to promote mutual understanding and support.

Addressing the legacy of slavery and systemic racism requires a comprehensive and sustained effort that includes education, advocacy, policy reforms, community engagement, and international solidarity. By recognizing the profound impact of slavery and supporting efforts for justice and reconciliation, societies can move towards a more equitable and inclusive future.

Chapter 7: Forms of Racism

Racism manifests in many forms, from overt acts of discrimination to subtle microaggressions and systemic inequalities. Understanding these different forms is crucial for recognizing and addressing racism in all its manifestations. This chapter explores the various types of racism, providing examples and discussing their impacts on individuals and society.

Overt Racism

Overt racism is the most visible and explicit form of racial discrimination. It includes blatant acts of prejudice and discrimination, such as hate speech, racial slurs, and physical violence. Overt racism is often rooted in the belief in the superiority of one race over another and can manifest in both individual actions and institutional policies.

Hate Crimes: Hate crimes are a glaring example of overt racism. These crimes are motivated by racial hatred and can range from verbal harassment to physical assault and even murder. High-profile cases, such as the 2015 Charleston church shooting in the United States, where nine African American churchgoers were killed by a white supremacist, highlight the extreme violence that overt racism can entail.

Discriminatory Laws: Overt racism can also be institutionalized through discriminatory laws and policies. For instance, apartheid in South Africa was a system of overt racial segregation and discrimination enforced by law. Similarly, the Jim Crow laws in the United States legally enforced racial segregation and disenfranchised Black Americans for decades.

Covert Racism

Covert racism, also known as hidden or subtle racism, is less visible but equally damaging. It involves discriminatory practices and attitudes that are not openly acknowledged or recognized. Covert racism can be intentional or unintentional and often operates through implicit biases and stereotypes.

Implicit Bias: Implicit bias refers to the unconscious attitudes and beliefs that individuals hold about different racial groups. These biases can influence behaviour and decision-making, often leading to discriminatory outcomes even when individuals are not consciously aware of their prejudices. For example, studies have shown that job applicants with ethnic-sounding names are less likely to be called for interviews compared to those with white-sounding names, even when their qualifications are identical.

Microaggressions: Microaggressions are everyday verbal, nonverbal, and environmental slights or insults that communicate hostile or negative messages to people based on their race. Microaggressions can be subtle and may seem harmless to the perpetrator, but they can have a cumulative and damaging impact on the recipient. Examples of microaggressions include a person of colour being repeatedly asked, "Where are you really from?" or being told, "You're so articulate" in a tone that implies surprise.

Systemic Racism

Systemic racism, also known as institutional or structural racism, refers to the policies and practices embedded within institutions that produce and perpetuate racial inequalities. This form of racism is deeply ingrained in the fabric of society and affects multiple aspects of life, including education, employment, healthcare, and housing.

Education: Systemic racism in education can be seen in the disparities in funding and resources available to schools serving predominantly minority communities. These schools often have fewer resources, less experienced teachers, and lower academic outcomes compared to schools in wealthier, predominantly white areas. This educational inequality contributes to the achievement gap and limits the opportunities available to students of colour.

Healthcare: In the healthcare system, systemic racism manifests in the disparities in access to care and health outcomes for different racial groups. Minority patients often receive lower-quality care and face barriers to accessing healthcare services. For example, Black women in the United States are more likely to die from pregnancy-related complications than white women, a disparity that persists regardless of income or education level.

Criminal Justice: The criminal justice system is another area where systemic racism is prevalent. Racial disparities in arrest rates, sentencing, and incarceration highlight the unequal treatment of people of colour. The over-policing of minority communities and the disproportionate impact of the war on drugs on Black and Latino individuals are stark examples of systemic racism in action.

Cultural Racism

Cultural racism refers to the societal beliefs and practices that promote the idea that the culture and values of one racial group are superior to those of another. This form of racism is perpetuated through media representations, cultural norms, and institutional practices that marginalize and devalue the contributions and identities of minority groups.

Media Representations: Media representations play a significant role in shaping societal attitudes and perceptions. Stereotypical portrayals of racial and ethnic minorities in movies, television shows, and news reports can reinforce harmful stereotypes and contribute to the marginalization of these groups. For instance, the portrayal of Black individuals as criminals or Latinos as illegal immigrants perpetuates negative stereotypes that influence public perception and policy.

Cultural Appropriation: Cultural appropriation is another aspect of cultural racism. It involves the adoption or exploitation of elements of a minority culture by members of a dominant culture without understanding or respecting the original context. This can include the use of traditional clothing, hairstyles, music, and other cultural expressions in ways that trivialize their significance.

Internalized Racism

Internalized racism occurs when individuals from marginalized racial groups accept and internalize the negative beliefs and stereotypes about their own group. This can lead to feelings of inferiority, low self-esteem, and self-hatred. Internalized racism is a result of the pervasive and insidious nature of systemic and cultural racism.

Self-Perception: Internalized racism can affect how individuals perceive themselves and their worth. This can manifest in preferences for lighter skin, straighter hair, and other traits associated with the dominant racial group. These preferences are often reinforced by societal standards of beauty and success that privilege whiteness.

Community Impact: Internalized racism can also affect how individuals relate to their own communities. It can lead to divisions within racial groups and a lack of solidarity in the fight against racism. Overcoming internalized racism involves fostering a sense of pride and resilience within marginalized communities and promoting positive representations of their cultures and identities.

Addressing and Combating Racism

Addressing the various forms of racism requires a multifaceted approach that includes education, policy reforms, and community engagement. It involves recognizing and challenging our own biases, advocating for systemic changes, and promoting a culture of inclusion and respect.

Education: Education is a powerful tool for combating racism. Schools and universities must provide curricula that reflect the diversity of experiences and contributions of all racial and ethnic groups. This includes teaching about the history of racism, the impact of slavery and colonialism, and the ongoing struggles for justice and equality.

Policy Reforms: Policy reforms are essential for addressing systemic racism. This includes implementing policies that promote equity in education, healthcare, employment, and housing. Legal protections against discrimination must be robustly enforced, and institutions must be held accountable for practices that perpetuate racial inequalities.

Community Engagement: Community engagement and grassroots activism play a crucial role in driving social change. Organizations and movements that advocate for racial justice, such as Black Lives Matter, the NAACP, and other civil rights groups, are vital in raising awareness, mobilizing communities, and pushing for policy changes.

Promoting Inclusion: Promoting a culture of inclusion involves creating environments where all individuals feel valued and respected. This includes fostering diversity in workplaces, educational institutions, and public spaces, and addressing cultural biases and stereotypes. Initiatives that promote cross-cultural understanding and dialogue can help to break down barriers and build solidarity.

Understanding the different manifestations of racism is crucial for recognizing and addressing them in our efforts to create a more inclusive world. This section will delve deeper into the nuanced and often insidious ways that racism can permeate society, highlighting the need for comprehensive strategies to combat it.

Structural Racism

Structural racism refers to the cumulative and compounding effects of an array of societal factors, including the history, culture, ideology, and interactions of institutions and policies that systematically privilege white people and disadvantage people of colour. Unlike systemic racism, which is embedded in specific institutions, structural racism spans across multiple institutions and systems, creating a web of interconnected barriers.

Housing: Structural racism in housing can be seen in practices such as redlining, zoning laws, and discriminatory lending practices. Redlining, the practice of denying mortgages or insurance to people based on the racial composition of their neighbourhood, has historically prevented people of colour from accumulating wealth through homeownership. Even today, people of colour are more likely to be denied mortgages or offered less favourable loan terms compared to their white counterparts with similar financial profiles.

Employment: In the labour market, structural racism manifests in hiring practices, wage disparities, and occupational segregation. People of colour often face discrimination in hiring processes, leading to higher unemployment rates and lower wages. Occupational segregation, where certain jobs are predominantly filled by people of a particular race, can limit economic mobility and perpetuate income disparities.

Education: In education, structural racism results in disparities in school funding, access to advanced coursework, and disciplinary practices. Schools in predominantly minority neighbourhoods are often underfunded, leading to larger class sizes, fewer resources, and lower academic outcomes. Disciplinary practices that disproportionately affect students of colour contribute to the school-to-prison pipeline, where marginalized students are funnelled out of the educational system and into the criminal justice system.

Healthcare: Structural racism in healthcare is evident in the disparities in health outcomes and access to care. People of colour often face barriers to accessing quality healthcare, resulting in higher rates of chronic illnesses and lower life expectancy. Implicit biases among healthcare providers can lead to differential treatment and poorer health outcomes for minority patients.

Everyday Racism

Everyday racism, also known as casual racism, encompasses the routine, normalized aspects of racism that individuals encounter in their daily lives. These experiences, while often subtle, can have a profound impact on an individual's mental and emotional well-being.

Microaggressions: Microaggressions are a common form of everyday racism. These can be verbal, nonverbal, or environmental slights that convey derogatory or negative messages to individuals based on their race. Examples include being followed around a store by security, being mistaken for a service worker, or being subjected to racial jokes and stereotypes. While each instance may seem minor, the cumulative effect of microaggressions can be deeply damaging.

Exclusion: Everyday racism can also manifest as social exclusion, where individuals of colour are systematically excluded from certain social or professional networks. This can limit their opportunities for advancement and contribute to feelings of isolation and alienation. For example, people of colour may be left out of informal workplace gatherings or social events, impacting their ability to build professional relationships and advance in their careers.

Cultural Insensitivity: Cultural insensitivity, where individuals or institutions fail to recognize and respect the cultural practices and traditions of minority groups, is another form of everyday racism. This can include mispronouncing or making fun of ethnic names, dismissing cultural practices as "strange" or "exotic," and failing to accommodate cultural or religious needs in the workplace or public spaces.

Colourism

Colourism, a form of discrimination based on skin colour, often occurs within racial and ethnic groups as well as between them. Lighter-skinned individuals are frequently afforded more privileges and opportunities compared to their darker-skinned counterparts. This preference for lighter skin can be traced back to colonialism and slavery, where lighter-skinned individuals were often given preferential treatment.

Impact on Individuals: Colourism can impact individuals' self-esteem and mental health, as they may internalize societal preferences for lighter skin and feel devalued or inferior. This can lead to practices such as skin bleaching, which pose significant health risks.

Social and Economic Consequences: Colourism also has social and economic consequences, influencing employment opportunities, educational attainment, and social mobility. Studies have shown that lighter-skinned individuals often have higher incomes and better job prospects compared to darker-skinned individuals within the same racial or ethnic group.

Xenophobia

Xenophobia, the fear or hatred of foreigners, often intersects with racism and can lead to discrimination against individuals based on their perceived foreignness. This can affect immigrants, refugees, and even citizens who are perceived as "other" due to their ethnic background or cultural practices.

Immigration Policies: Xenophobia can influence immigration policies, leading to restrictive laws and practices that disproportionately affect people from certain regions or ethnic backgrounds. These policies can result in family separations, detention, and deportation, contributing to the marginalization and vulnerability of immigrant communities.

Social Exclusion: Xenophobic attitudes can also lead to social exclusion and discrimination in everyday interactions. Immigrants and refugees may face hostility, prejudice, and violence in their host countries, impacting their ability to integrate and access essential services.

Intersectionality

Intersectionality is a framework for understanding how multiple social identities, such as race, gender, class, and sexuality, intersect and contribute to unique experiences of oppression and privilege. Coined by legal scholar

Kimberlé Crenshaw, intersectionality emphasizes that individuals experience discrimination in overlapping and interconnected ways.

Multiple Forms of Oppression: For example, a Black woman may face discrimination based on both her race and gender, leading to experiences that are distinct from those of Black men or white women. Recognizing these intersecting identities is crucial for addressing the full complexity of individuals' experiences and developing more effective strategies for combating discrimination.

Inclusive Policies and Practices: Addressing intersectionality requires inclusive policies and practices that consider the multiple dimensions of individuals' identities. This includes ensuring that anti-discrimination laws and initiatives are comprehensive and address the specific needs of marginalized groups.

Addressing and Combating Racism

To effectively combat the various forms of racism, it is essential to adopt a multifaceted approach that includes education, policy reforms, community engagement, and individual action.

Education: Comprehensive education about the history and impact of racism is vital for raising awareness and promoting understanding. This includes integrating diverse perspectives into curricula and providing training on cultural competence and implicit bias.

Policy Reforms: Policy reforms should aim to address systemic and structural inequalities across all areas of society. This includes equitable funding for education, healthcare access, criminal justice reform, and economic policies that promote wealth-building opportunities for marginalized communities.

Community Engagement: Grassroots activism and community engagement are crucial for driving social change and holding institutions accountable. Supporting organizations that advocate for racial justice and creating spaces for dialogue and solidarity can help to build more inclusive communities.

Individual Action: Individuals can also play a role in combating racism by examining their own biases, speaking out against discrimination, and promoting inclusive practices in their personal and professional lives. By taking responsibility for their actions and advocating for change, individuals can contribute to a broader movement for racial justice.

Chapter 8: Institutional Racism

Institutional racism, also known as systemic racism, refers to the policies and practices within institutions that systematically disadvantage certain racial groups. Unlike individual acts of prejudice, institutional racism is embedded in the very fabric of our social, political, and economic systems. It is pervasive, often invisible, and its effects are far-reaching and enduring. In this chapter, we will explore the nature of institutional racism, its manifestations in various sectors, and the efforts being made to dismantle it.

Defining Institutional Racism

Institutional racism occurs when the policies, practices, and procedures of an institution create or perpetuate racial inequalities. These disparities can manifest in various domains, including education, healthcare, housing, criminal justice, and employment. Institutional racism is often subtle and indirect, making it difficult to identify and address. It operates through norms and structures that appear neutral but disproportionately harm marginalized communities.

Historical Roots: Institutional racism has deep historical roots. Many of the policies and practices that continue to disadvantage people of color today were established during periods of explicit racial segregation and discrimination. The legacy of slavery, colonialism, and segregation has left a lasting imprint on institutions, perpetuating inequality across generations.

Mechanisms of Institutional Racism: Institutional racism operates through several mechanisms:
- Discriminatory Policies: Policies that explicitly or implicitly discriminate against certain racial groups.
- Bias in Decision-Making: Decisions made by individuals within institutions that reflect conscious or unconscious biases.

- Resource Allocation: Unequal distribution of resources that disproportionately benefits certain racial groups over others.
- Cultural Norms: Institutional cultures that normalize and perpetuate racial stereotypes and biases.

Manifestations in Different Sectors

Education: Institutional racism in education can be seen in the unequal distribution of resources, discriminatory disciplinary practices, and biased curricula.
- Funding Disparities: Schools in predominantly minority neighborhoods often receive less funding than those in affluent, predominantly white areas. This funding gap leads to disparities in facilities, educational materials, and extracurricular opportunities.
- Disciplinary Practices: Students of color, particularly Black and Latino students, are more likely to be suspended, expelled, or referred to law enforcement for disciplinary issues compared to their white peers. These practices contribute to the school-to-prison pipeline.
- Curriculum Bias: Many educational curricula fail to adequately represent the histories and contributions of marginalized communities, perpetuating a Eurocentric perspective.

Healthcare: In healthcare, institutional racism contributes to significant disparities in health outcomes and access to care.
- Access to Healthcare: People of color often face barriers to accessing quality healthcare, including lack of

insurance, geographic barriers, and discriminatory practices by healthcare providers.
- Health Disparities: Minority communities experience higher rates of chronic diseases, infant mortality, and mental health issues. These disparities are exacerbated by socioeconomic factors and systemic neglect.
- Implicit Bias: Healthcare providers may hold implicit biases that affect their treatment decisions, leading to unequal care for patients of different racial backgrounds.

Housing: Institutional racism in housing is evident in discriminatory lending practices, segregation, and unequal access to affordable housing.
- Redlining: Historically, redlining policies denied loans and insurance to residents in predominantly minority neighborhoods, leading to disinvestment and decay in these areas. The effects of redlining are still felt today, with persistent segregation and economic disparities.
- Predatory Lending: Minority homebuyers are more likely to receive subprime loans with higher interest rates and unfavourable terms, contributing to higher rates of foreclosure and financial instability.
- Housing Segregation: Zoning laws and discriminatory practices in the housing market perpetuate residential segregation, limiting access to quality education, healthcare, and employment opportunities for people of color.

Criminal Justice: The criminal justice system is a significant site of institutional racism, with disparities in policing, sentencing, and incarceration rates.

- Policing Practices: People of color, particularly Black individuals, are disproportionately targeted by police for stops, searches, and arrests. Practices such as racial profiling and "stop-and-frisk" policies contribute to these disparities.
- Sentencing Disparities: Racial biases in sentencing lead to harsher penalties for people of color compared to white individuals for similar offenses. This contributes to the overrepresentation of minorities in the prison system.
- Mass Incarceration: The war on drugs and tough-on-crime policies have disproportionately affected communities of color, leading to high rates of incarceration and significant social and economic consequences for these communities.

Employment: Institutional racism in employment manifests in hiring practices, wage disparities, and workplace discrimination.
- Hiring Bias: Studies have shown that resumes with traditionally white-sounding names receive more callbacks than those with names associated with people of color, indicating bias in the hiring process.
- Wage Gaps: People of color, particularly Black and Latino workers, often earn less than their white counterparts for similar work. This wage gap contributes to economic disparities and limits opportunities for upward mobility.
- Workplace Discrimination: Discriminatory practices in the workplace, such as unequal access to promotions, biased performance evaluations, and hostile work environments, perpetuate inequality and limit career advancement for people of color.

Efforts to Address Institutional Racism

Addressing institutional racism requires comprehensive and sustained efforts across all sectors of society. These efforts involve policy reforms, institutional changes, and community initiatives aimed at promoting equity and inclusion.

Policy Reforms: Implementing and enforcing anti-discrimination laws and policies is crucial for addressing institutional racism. This includes:
- Affirmative Action: Policies that promote the inclusion of underrepresented groups in education and employment can help address historical disparities and create more diverse institutions.
- Criminal Justice Reform: Reforms aimed at reducing racial disparities in policing, sentencing, and incarceration, such as ending mandatory minimum sentences and promoting alternatives to incarceration.
- Healthcare Equity: Policies that expand access to healthcare for marginalized communities and address social determinants of health, such as housing and education.

Institutional Changes: Institutions must take proactive steps to dismantle systemic racism within their structures. This involves:
- Diversity and Inclusion Initiatives: Implementing programs and practices that promote diversity, equity, and inclusion within the institution. This includes bias

training, diversity recruitment efforts, and creating inclusive work environments.
- Accountability Mechanisms: Establishing mechanisms to hold institutions accountable for their diversity and inclusion efforts, such as regular audits, reporting requirements, and oversight bodies.
- Community Engagement: Building partnerships with marginalized communities to understand their needs and perspectives and involving them in decision-making processes.

Community Initiatives: Grassroots efforts and community-led initiatives play a crucial role in addressing institutional racism. These include:
- Advocacy and Activism: Supporting organizations and movements that advocate for racial justice and systemic change. This includes participating in protests, campaigns, and advocacy efforts.
- Education and Awareness: Raising awareness about institutional racism and its impact through education programs, public awareness campaigns, and community events.
- Support Services: Providing support services for marginalized communities, such as legal aid, housing assistance, and mental health resources, to address immediate needs and promote long-term stability.

Continuing our examination of institutional racism, we will delve into specific case studies that illustrate how systemic inequities manifest in various sectors. These case studies will highlight the experiences of marginalized communities and the ongoing efforts to challenge and dismantle institutional racism.

 Case Study: Education

The Disparities in School Funding

One of the most glaring examples of institutional racism in education is the disparity in school funding. In many countries, public schools are funded through local property taxes, which inherently benefits schools in affluent, predominantly white neighborhoods and disadvantages those in poorer, predominantly minority neighborhoods.

Impact on Resources and Opportunities: Schools in underfunded areas often lack basic resources such as textbooks, technology, and extracurricular programs. These disparities create an unequal educational experience that limits opportunities for students of color. Without access to quality education, students are less prepared for higher education and competitive job markets.

Efforts for Reform: Efforts to address these disparities include campaigns for equitable funding formulas, such as those proposed by the Education Law Centre in the United States. Some states have implemented reforms to ensure more equitable distribution of funds, though significant disparities remain. Advocates continue to push for policies that would allocate resources based on student need rather than property wealth.

Case Study: Healthcare

Racial Disparities in Maternal Health

Racial disparities in maternal health outcomes are a stark example of institutional racism in healthcare. Black women in the United States, for instance, are three to four times more likely to die from pregnancy-related causes than white women. These disparities are not solely due to socioeconomic factors but also reflect systemic biases in healthcare delivery.

Factors Contributing to Disparities: Implicit bias among healthcare providers, inadequate access to prenatal care, and the stress associated with systemic racism all contribute to poorer maternal health outcomes for Black women. Research has shown that Black women often receive lower quality care and are less likely to be listened to by healthcare providers.

Initiatives for Change: Various initiatives aim to address these disparities. Programs like the Black Mamas Matter Alliance advocate for improved maternal health policies, provide community support, and raise awareness about the issues. Hospitals and healthcare systems are also implementing bias training for providers and developing protocols to ensure equitable care for all patients.

Case Study: Housing

The Legacy of Redlining

Redlining, the discriminatory practice of denying services such as mortgages or insurance to residents of certain areas based on their race, has had long-lasting effects on housing segregation and economic inequality. Although outlawed in the United States by the Fair Housing Act of 1968, the impacts of redlining are still evident today.

Effects on Communities: Redlined communities, predominantly inhabited by people of color, have faced decades of disinvestment. This has resulted in lower property values, underfunded schools, and limited economic opportunities. The lack of investment in these areas has perpetuated cycles of poverty and segregation.

Current Efforts to Address Housing Inequality: Efforts to rectify these disparities include programs aimed at increasing homeownership among people of color, revitalizing neglected neighborhoods, and enforcing fair housing laws. Organizations like the National Community Reinvestment Coalition work to promote access to fair credit and investment in underserved communities.

Case Study: Criminal Justice

Racial Disparities in Sentencing

The criminal justice system's racial disparities are stark, particularly in sentencing practices. Black and Latino individuals often receive harsher sentences than their white counterparts for similar offenses. This systemic bias contributes to the overrepresentation of people of color in prisons and jails.

Mandatory Minimum Sentences: Policies such as mandatory minimum sentences for drug offenses have disproportionately affected Black and Latino communities. These policies remove judicial discretion and often result in lengthy prison terms for non-violent offenses.

Reform Initiatives: Criminal justice reform efforts focus on reducing these disparities through policy changes and advocacy. The Sentencing Project, for example, advocates for the elimination of mandatory minimum sentences, the implementation of fair sentencing laws, and the promotion of alternatives to incarceration.

Case Study: Employment

Bias in Hiring Practices

Institutional racism in employment is evident in biased hiring practices that disadvantage people of color. Studies have shown that resumes with names perceived as traditionally Black or Latino are less likely to receive callbacks than those with white-sounding names, even when qualifications are identical.

Wage Disparities and Advancement Opportunities: People of color often face wage disparities and limited opportunities for advancement within their careers.

These disparities contribute to the racial wealth gap and limit economic mobility.

Addressing Employment Inequities: Organizations are working to address these issues through diversity and inclusion initiatives. Companies are being encouraged to implement blind hiring practices, provide bias training for hiring managers, and set diversity goals. Additionally, advocacy groups push for policies that promote equal pay and support career advancement for marginalized groups.

 Moving Forward: Strategies for Dismantling Institutional Racism

Addressing institutional racism requires a multifaceted approach that involves policy changes, institutional reforms, and community initiatives. The following strategies are essential for dismantling systemic inequities and promoting racial justice:

Policy Changes:
- Comprehensive Anti-Discrimination Laws: Strengthening and enforcing laws that prohibit discrimination in housing, employment, education, and healthcare.
- Equitable Funding Policies: Implementing funding formulas that allocate resources based on need rather than property wealth, particularly in education and healthcare.

- Criminal Justice Reform: Eliminating mandatory minimum sentences, promoting alternatives to incarceration, and ensuring fair sentencing practices.

Institutional Reforms:
- Bias Training and Education: Providing ongoing training for individuals within institutions to recognize and address implicit biases.
- Accountability Mechanisms: Establishing oversight bodies and regular audits to ensure that institutions are held accountable for their diversity and inclusion efforts.
- Inclusive Practices: Implementing policies that promote diversity, equity, and inclusion within institutions, such as equitable hiring practices and support for minority employees.

Community Initiatives:
- Grassroots Advocacy: Supporting local organizations and movements that advocate for racial justice and systemic change.
- Public Awareness Campaigns: Raising awareness about institutional racism and its impacts through education programs and media campaigns.
- Support Services: Providing resources and support for marginalized communities, including legal aid, housing assistance, and healthcare services.

As we continue to explore the far-reaching impact of institutional racism, it is important to examine how these systemic inequities affect specific communities and what strategies are being employed to address and dismantle them. This page will focus on the intersectionality of institutional racism and its impact on marginalized groups, including women of color, immigrants, and indigenous peoples. By understanding these intersections, we can develop more comprehensive and effective solutions.

Intersectionality and Institutional Racism

Intersectionality is a framework for understanding how various aspects of a person's identity—such as race, gender, class, and sexuality—intersect and interact to create unique experiences of discrimination and privilege. Institutional racism does not operate in isolation; it intersects with other forms of systemic oppression, compounding the disadvantages faced by marginalized groups.

Women of Color: Women of color experience the combined effects of racism and sexism, which manifest in various ways across different sectors.
- Workplace Discrimination: Women of color often face barriers to advancement in the workplace, including lower wages, limited career opportunities, and workplace harassment. Studies have shown that women of color are less likely to be promoted and more likely to experience pay inequity compared to their white counterparts.
- Healthcare Inequities: In healthcare, women of color encounter disparities in access to care and health outcomes. For instance, Black women have higher rates of maternal mortality and breast cancer mortality compared to white women, due to a combination of

systemic bias, lack of access to quality healthcare, and socio-economic factors.

Immigrants: Immigrants, particularly those from non-European countries, face institutional racism that affects their integration and opportunities within society.
- Employment Barriers: Immigrants often encounter obstacles in the job market, such as credential recognition issues, language barriers, and discriminatory hiring practices. These barriers limit their economic opportunities and contribute to higher rates of underemployment and poverty.
- Legal Challenges: Immigrants may also face legal discrimination, including restrictive immigration policies and unequal access to legal protections. This can lead to exploitation, fear of deportation, and limited access to public services.

Indigenous Peoples: Indigenous peoples worldwide experience the enduring impacts of colonization and systemic racism, which affect their rights, resources, and opportunities.
- Land and Resource Rights: Indigenous communities often struggle to secure land and resource rights, facing legal and political challenges that stem from historical dispossession. These issues impact their ability to maintain cultural practices, economic self-sufficiency, and environmental stewardship.
- Health Disparities: Indigenous peoples face significant health disparities, including higher rates of chronic diseases, mental health issues, and lower life expectancy.

These disparities are linked to socio-economic determinants, systemic neglect, and historical trauma.

Strategies for Addressing Intersectional Racism

Addressing the intersectional nature of institutional racism requires targeted strategies that consider the unique challenges faced by different marginalized groups. The following approaches highlight some of the ways institutions and communities are working to address these complex issues.

Targeted Policy Reforms:
- Equal Pay and Advancement: Policies aimed at closing the wage gap and promoting career advancement for women of color are crucial. This includes implementing pay equity laws, mandating diversity in hiring and promotion practices, and providing support for professional development.
- Inclusive Healthcare Policies: Healthcare policies should prioritize equitable access and outcomes for marginalized groups, such as expanding coverage for prenatal care for women of color and ensuring culturally competent care for all patients. Programs that address social determinants of health and provide community-based services are essential.

Support for Immigrants:
- Employment Programs: Initiatives that support the economic integration of immigrants, such as job training programs, language education, and credential recognition services, can help overcome barriers to employment.

Employers should be encouraged to recognize the value of diverse workforces and implement inclusive hiring practices.
- Legal Advocacy: Legal support services for immigrants, including pro bono legal aid and advocacy for fair immigration policies, are crucial for protecting their rights and ensuring access to justice. Organizations that work to reform immigration laws and policies play a vital role in this effort.

Empowerment of Indigenous Communities:
- Land Rights and Environmental Justice: Supporting Indigenous land rights and environmental justice initiatives is critical. This includes advocating for legal recognition of land claims, protecting sacred sites, and promoting sustainable development practices that respect Indigenous knowledge and traditions.
- Cultural Revitalization Programs: Programs that support the revitalization of Indigenous languages, cultural practices, and governance structures can help strengthen community resilience and identity. These initiatives should be led by Indigenous communities and supported by adequate funding and resources.

Case Study: Indigenous Land Rights in Canada

In Canada, the fight for Indigenous land rights has been a central issue in the broader struggle against institutional racism. The landmark Supreme Court case of Tsilhqot'in Nation v. British Columbia (2014) recognized the Tsilhqot'in people's Aboriginal title to their traditional territory, setting a precedent for future land claims.

Impact of the Tsilhqot'in Decision: This decision affirmed the right of Indigenous peoples to control the use of their land and resources, providing a legal foundation for challenging unauthorized development projects. It also highlighted the importance of respecting Indigenous sovereignty and engaging in meaningful consultation and consent processes.

Ongoing Challenges: Despite this progress, many Indigenous communities continue to face challenges in securing land rights and protecting their territories from exploitation. Efforts to implement the United Nations Declaration on the Rights of Indigenous Peoples (UNDRIP) into Canadian law are ongoing, with advocates pushing for stronger legal frameworks and enforcement mechanisms.

Community-Led Initiatives

Community-led initiatives are essential for addressing institutional racism and supporting marginalized groups. These initiatives leverage local knowledge and resources to create tailored solutions that meet the specific needs of the community.

Grassroots Organizations: Grassroots organizations play a crucial role in advocating for systemic change and providing support services. Examples include:
- Black Lives Matter (BLM): BLM chapters across the globe work to combat police brutality, racial profiling,

and systemic racism through advocacy, education, and community organizing.
- Migrant Rights Organizations: Groups like the National Immigration Law Centre (NILC) and Migrant Rights Network advocate for immigrant rights, provide legal assistance, and push for inclusive policies.

Community Health Programs: Health initiatives led by and for marginalized communities can address specific health disparities and promote wellness. Examples include:
- Indigenous Health Programs: Indigenous-led health organizations, such as the First Nations Health Authority in Canada, provide culturally appropriate healthcare services and promote holistic approaches to health and wellness.

Educational Empowerment: Community-based education programs that focus on empowerment and advocacy can help address institutional racism. Examples include:
- Educational Equity Initiatives: Programs that provide tutoring, mentorship, and college preparation support for students of color can help bridge the educational achievement gap.

As we move forward in our discussion of institutional racism, it is important to explore the global dimensions of this issue. Institutional racism is not confined to any one country; it manifests in various forms around the world. By examining international examples, we can gain a deeper understanding of how systemic racism operates globally and identify common strategies for combating it.

Institutional Racism in a Global Context

Australia: The treatment of Indigenous Australians provides a stark example of institutional racism. Policies of dispossession, assimilation, and discrimination have profoundly affected Indigenous communities, leading to significant disparities in health, education, and economic outcomes.

Historical Policies of Dispossession: The colonization of Australia involved the systematic dispossession of Indigenous lands, which disrupted traditional ways of life and led to social and economic marginalization. Policies such as the forcible removal of children, known as the Stolen Generations, aimed to assimilate Indigenous people into white society, causing lasting trauma and loss of cultural identity.

Contemporary Issues: Today, Indigenous Australians face significant disadvantages, including lower life expectancy, higher rates of incarceration, and poorer health outcomes compared to the non-Indigenous population. Efforts to address these disparities include the Close the Gap campaign, which aims to achieve health equality, and various initiatives focused on land rights and cultural preservation.

South Africa: The legacy of apartheid continues to shape the socio-economic landscape of South Africa, with institutional racism deeply entrenched in the country's institutions and systems.

Apartheid's Legacy: The apartheid regime implemented strict racial segregation laws that marginalized Black South Africans and limited their access to education, healthcare, and economic opportunities. Although apartheid officially ended in 1994, its effects persist, with significant racial disparities in wealth, education, and living conditions.

Post-Apartheid Challenges: Efforts to redress these inequalities include affirmative action policies, land reform programs, and social welfare initiatives. However, challenges remain, such as corruption, economic instability, and ongoing racial tensions. The work of organizations like the Nelson Mandela Foundation and the South African Human Rights Commission is crucial in promoting social justice and reconciliation.

Brazil: Brazil's history of slavery and its ongoing racial inequalities provide another example of institutional racism on a global scale.

Slavery's Enduring Impact: Brazil was the last country in the Americas to abolish slavery, in 1888. The legacy of slavery continues to affect Afro-Brazilians, who face higher rates of poverty, lower levels of education, and limited access to quality healthcare and employment opportunities.

Affirmative Action and Quotas: In recent years, Brazil has implemented affirmative action policies, including racial quotas in public universities and government jobs, to address these disparities. These measures have had some success in increasing representation and opportunities for Afro-Brazilians, but significant challenges remain in fully dismantling systemic racism.

Global Strategies for Combating Institutional Racism

International Human Rights Frameworks: International organizations, such as the United Nations, play a crucial role in promoting human rights and addressing systemic racism globally. Instruments like the International Convention on the Elimination of All Forms of Racial Discrimination (ICERD) provide a framework for countries to combat racism and promote equality.

Global Advocacy Campaigns: Global advocacy campaigns, such as the International Decade for People of African Descent (2015-2024), aim to raise awareness about racial discrimination and promote actions to address it. These campaigns encourage international cooperation and the sharing of best practices.

Transnational Solidarity: Building transnational solidarity among marginalized communities and activists can strengthen the global movement against institutional racism. By sharing strategies, resources, and experiences, activists can support each other's efforts and amplify their impact.

Research and Data Collection: Conducting research and collecting data on racial disparities is essential for understanding the scope of institutional racism and developing effective interventions. International collaborations among researchers, governments, and non-governmental organizations can help build a comprehensive picture of global racial inequalities.

 Case Study: The International Decade for People of African Descent

The United Nations declared 2015-2024 as the International Decade for People of African Descent, recognizing the need to address the historical and contemporary injustices faced by people of African descent worldwide.

Goals and Objectives: The Decade aims to promote recognition, justice, and development for people of African descent. Its key objectives include promoting respect, protection, and fulfilment of all human rights and fundamental freedoms by people of African descent, and strengthening national, regional, and international legal frameworks.

Key Initiatives: Initiatives under the Decade include:
- Education and Awareness: Promoting the contributions of people of African descent to society and addressing the history of slavery and colonialism in educational curricula.

- Legal and Policy Reforms: Encouraging countries to adopt and implement anti-discrimination laws and policies that address systemic racism.
- Economic Empowerment: Supporting economic development programs that address the disparities faced by people of African descent and promote equitable access to resources and opportunities.

Impact and Challenges: While the Decade has raised awareness and led to some positive changes, challenges remain in achieving its goals. These include political resistance, limited resources, and the need for greater international cooperation. Continued advocacy and commitment are essential for sustaining progress.

Moving Forward: Global Solidarity and Local Action

Combating institutional racism requires both global solidarity and local action. While international frameworks and collaborations are crucial, the implementation of effective strategies must be tailored to the specific contexts and needs of local communities.

Localizing Global Strategies: Adapting global strategies to local contexts involves understanding the unique challenges faced by marginalized communities and developing culturally appropriate interventions. This requires active engagement with local stakeholders, including community leaders, activists, and affected individuals.

Empowering Local Communities: Empowering local communities to take action against institutional racism involves providing resources, support, and platforms for advocacy. Community-led initiatives are often the most effective in addressing specific local issues and driving sustainable change.

Building International Alliances: Building alliances between local and international organizations can enhance the effectiveness of efforts to combat institutional racism. These alliances facilitate the exchange of knowledge, resources, and best practices, and amplify the voices of marginalized communities on a global stage.

In this concluding section, we will explore the role of education, advocacy, and technology in addressing institutional racism. By leveraging these tools, we can create more effective and sustainable strategies for promoting equity and dismantling systemic barriers.

The Role of Education in Combating Institutional Racism

Education is a powerful tool in the fight against institutional racism. By educating individuals and communities about the history and impact of systemic racism, we can foster greater understanding, empathy, and commitment to change.

Inclusive Curriculum: Developing and implementing an inclusive curriculum that accurately reflects the histories

and contributions of marginalized communities is crucial. This includes:
- Historical Context: Teaching about the history of racism, including slavery, colonization, segregation, and the civil rights movements, helps students understand the roots and enduring impact of systemic racism.
- Cultural Contributions: Highlighting the contributions of people of color to society, including achievements in science, arts, politics, and social movements, fosters a more comprehensive and inclusive understanding of history.

Anti-Racist Education: Integrating anti-racist education into school curricula helps students recognize and challenge racism in their own lives and communities.
- Critical Thinking: Encouraging students to critically examine societal structures and their own biases promotes a deeper understanding of how racism operates and how it can be dismantled.
- Empathy and Action: Teaching students about the experiences of marginalized groups and encouraging them to take action against injustice fosters empathy and a commitment to social justice.

Professional Development for Educators: Providing educators with training on cultural competence, implicit bias, and anti-racist practices is essential for creating inclusive and equitable learning environments.
- Ongoing Training: Regular professional development opportunities help educators stay informed about best practices and emerging research in the field of anti-racist education.

- Supportive Resources: Access to resources, such as lesson plans, reading materials, and workshops, supports educators in their efforts to implement inclusive and anti-racist curricula.

The Role of Advocacy in Addressing Institutional Racism

Advocacy is a critical component of efforts to combat institutional racism. Through advocacy, individuals and organizations can push for policy changes, raise awareness, and hold institutions accountable.

Grassroots Advocacy: Grassroots advocacy involves community-led efforts to address local issues of racism and promote social justice.
- Community Organizing: Organizing community meetings, protests, and campaigns to raise awareness and advocate for change can mobilize support and create momentum for addressing systemic issues.
- Partnerships: Building partnerships with local organizations, faith groups, and other community stakeholders strengthens advocacy efforts and amplifies their impact.

Policy Advocacy: Policy advocacy focuses on influencing legislation and public policy to promote equity and address systemic racism.
- Legislative Reforms: Advocating for policies that promote equitable funding for education, healthcare, and housing, as well as criminal justice reform, is crucial for dismantling institutional racism.

- Lobbying and Campaigns: Engaging with policymakers, participating in lobbying efforts, and organizing public awareness campaigns can drive legislative change and ensure that the needs of marginalized communities are addressed.

Legal Advocacy: Legal advocacy involves using the legal system to challenge discriminatory practices and protect the rights of marginalized individuals.
- Litigation: Filing lawsuits against discriminatory practices and policies can lead to significant legal victories and set precedents for future cases.
- Legal Support: Providing legal assistance to individuals facing discrimination helps protect their rights and ensures access to justice.

 The Role of Technology in Combating Institutional Racism

Technology offers powerful tools for addressing institutional racism and promoting equity. By leveraging digital platforms, data analytics, and innovative solutions, we can enhance advocacy efforts and create more inclusive systems.

Digital Platforms for Advocacy: Social media and other digital platforms provide avenues for raising awareness, organizing campaigns, and mobilizing support.
- Awareness Campaigns: Using social media to share information, personal stories, and educational resources can raise awareness about institutional racism and its impact.

- Online Communities: Creating online communities and networks for activists and advocates fosters collaboration, support, and the sharing of strategies and resources.

Data Analytics: Data analytics can be used to identify disparities, track progress, and inform policy decisions.
- Identifying Disparities: Analyzing data on education, healthcare, employment, and criminal justice can reveal patterns of inequality and highlight areas in need of intervention.
- Evaluating Impact: Using data to evaluate the effectiveness of policies and programs helps ensure that efforts to address institutional racism are evidence-based and impactful.

Innovative Solutions: Technology can also be used to develop innovative solutions that promote equity and inclusion.
- Equity in Education: Online learning platforms and educational technologies can provide access to quality education for marginalized communities, addressing disparities in resources and opportunities.
- Healthcare Access: Telemedicine and digital health initiatives can improve access to healthcare for underserved populations, reducing barriers related to geography and availability of services.

Case Study: Using Technology to Address Racial Disparities in Healthcare

Project ECHO (Extension for Community Healthcare Outcomes): Project ECHO is an innovative telemedicine model that uses technology to expand access to specialized healthcare for underserved populations.
- Model: The ECHO model connects primary care providers in remote or underserved areas with specialists through virtual clinics, enabling them to receive training and support.
- Impact: By leveraging technology, Project ECHO has improved healthcare outcomes in areas such as hepatitis C treatment, mental health, and chronic disease management, particularly in marginalized communities.
- Scalability: The success of Project ECHO has led to its adoption in various countries and healthcare settings, demonstrating the potential of technology to address healthcare disparities on a global scale.

 Moving Forward: Integrating Education, Advocacy, and Technology

Combating institutional racism requires a holistic approach that integrates education, advocacy, and technology. By leveraging these tools, we can create more effective and sustainable strategies for promoting equity and dismantling systemic barriers.

Collaborative Efforts: Collaboration between educators, advocates, technologists, and policymakers is essential for addressing the complex and interconnected issues of institutional racism.

- Interdisciplinary Partnerships: Building partnerships across disciplines can foster innovative solutions and ensure that efforts are comprehensive and coordinated.
- Community Involvement: Engaging with communities and incorporating their perspectives and needs into initiatives helps ensure that efforts are relevant and impactful.

Sustained Commitment: Addressing institutional racism requires sustained commitment and ongoing efforts.
- Continuous Improvement: Regularly assessing and refining strategies based on feedback and outcomes helps ensure that efforts remain effective and responsive to changing needs.
- Long-Term Vision: Maintaining a long-term vision for equity and justice ensures that efforts are sustained, and progress is made over time.

Conclusion

Institutional racism is a pervasive and complex issue that requires a multifaceted approach to address. By leveraging the power of education, advocacy, and technology, we can develop more effective strategies for dismantling systemic barriers and promoting equity and inclusion. Collaborative efforts, sustained commitment, and a holistic approach are essential in the fight against institutional racism. Together, we can create a more just and equitable world for future generations.

Chapter 9: Hidden Racism

Hidden racism, also known as covert racism, refers to subtle and often unconscious forms of racial bias and discrimination that permeate everyday interactions and societal norms. Unlike overt racism, which is explicit and easily identifiable, hidden racism is insidious and can be more challenging to recognize and address. This chapter explores the various manifestations of hidden racism and its impact on individuals and communities.

Implicit Bias

Implicit bias involves unconscious attitudes and stereotypes that affect our understanding, actions, and decisions regarding different racial groups. These biases are deeply ingrained and can influence behaviour even when individuals consciously reject racist beliefs.

Impact on Decision-Making: Implicit biases can affect decision-making in numerous contexts, including hiring practices, law enforcement, healthcare, and education. For example, a hiring manager may unconsciously favour a white candidate over a more qualified candidate of color due to implicit biases. Similarly, healthcare providers might underestimate the pain levels of Black patients compared to white patients, leading to disparities in treatment.

Addressing Implicit Bias: Reducing implicit bias requires self-awareness and ongoing effort. Implicit bias training programs, which are designed to help individuals recognize and address their unconscious biases, are increasingly being implemented in workplaces, schools, and other institutions. These programs typically involve exercises and discussions aimed at uncovering hidden biases and promoting strategies to mitigate their impact.

Microaggressions

Microaggressions are brief, everyday exchanges that send denigrating messages to individuals based on their racial or ethnic identity. These can be verbal, nonverbal, or environmental and are often unintentional. However, their cumulative effect can be deeply harmful.

Types of Microaggressions: Microaggressions can take many forms, including micro assaults, microinsults, and microinvalidations. Micro assaults are explicit racial derogations, such as using racial slurs. Microinsults are subtle snubs or comments that convey disrespect, such as questioning a person's intelligence based on their race. Microinvalidations are statements or actions that exclude or negate the experiences of people of color, such as telling a Black person that racism no longer exists.

Impact on Mental Health: The cumulative effect of microaggressions can lead to significant stress and anxiety, affecting the mental health and well-being of individuals who experience them regularly. Over time, microaggressions can contribute to a hostile and unwelcoming environment, impacting academic and professional performance and personal relationships.

Colourblind Racism

Colourblind racism is the belief that ignoring or overlooking racial differences will lead to racial equality. While this approach may seem progressive, it often perpetuates racial disparities by failing to acknowledge and address the unique challenges faced by people of color.

Denial of Racism: Colour-blindness often involves denying the existence of racism and its impact on marginalized communities. This can manifest in statements like "I don't see color" or "We're all just human." Such statements, while well-intentioned, ignore the systemic and structural barriers that people of color face.

Maintaining the Status Quo: By refusing to recognize racial differences, colour-blindness can maintain the status quo and hinder efforts to address racial inequities. It allows individuals and institutions to avoid confronting their own biases and the broader societal structures that perpetuate racism.

Promoting Racial Equity: Instead of adopting a colourblind approach, promoting racial equity requires actively acknowledging and addressing racial disparities. This involves recognizing the unique experiences and challenges of different racial groups and implementing targeted strategies to promote inclusion and fairness.

Stereotype Threat

Stereotype threat refers to the anxiety and performance decrements that individuals may experience when they are aware of negative stereotypes about their racial group. This phenomenon can affect academic, professional, and personal performance, leading to a self-fulfilling prophecy.

Impact on Performance: When individuals are aware of stereotypes that question their abilities, such as the stereotype that Black students are less academically capable, they may experience increased stress and anxiety. This can impair their performance, reinforcing the negative stereotype and perpetuating a cycle of underachievement.

Addressing Stereotype Threat: Reducing stereotype threat involves creating supportive and inclusive environments that challenge negative stereotypes and promote positive self-affirmation. This can include providing mentorship and support networks, promoting diverse role models, and fostering a culture of growth and resilience.

Tokenism

Tokenism occurs when individuals from marginalized groups are included in an organization or group primarily to give the appearance of diversity and inclusion, rather than to genuinely value their contributions. Tokenism can create a superficial sense of diversity while failing to address underlying issues of inequality.

Isolation and Marginalization: Individuals who are tokenized may feel isolated and marginalized, as they are often expected to represent their entire racial or ethnic group. This can lead to feelings of tokenism, where their presence is more about fulfilling a diversity quota than valuing their unique perspectives and abilities.

True Inclusion: True inclusion involves creating an environment where diversity is genuinely valued and individuals from all backgrounds are supported and empowered to contribute fully. This requires moving beyond tokenism to implement meaningful diversity and inclusion initiatives that address systemic barriers and promote equity.

Institutional Practices

Hidden racism is often perpetuated through institutional practices that may not appear overtly discriminatory but nonetheless produce unequal outcomes for different racial groups.

Discriminatory Policies: Policies that disproportionately impact people of color, even if they are not explicitly racist, contribute to hidden racism. For example, school discipline policies that result in higher suspension rates for Black students can perpetuate educational inequities.

Unequal Access: Institutions may also engage in practices that limit access to resources and opportunities for marginalized groups. This can include unequal access to advanced coursework in schools, biased hiring practices, and limited representation in leadership positions.

Creating Equitable Institutions: Addressing hidden racism in institutional practices involves critically examining policies and procedures to identify and eliminate disparities. This can include conducting equity audits, implementing bias training, and developing inclusive policies that promote fairness and equity.

Addressing Hidden Racism

Addressing hidden racism requires a multifaceted approach that includes self-awareness, education, policy reforms, and community engagement. Key strategies include:

Self-Reflection: Individuals must engage in self-reflection to recognize and address their own biases. This involves being open to feedback, seeking out diverse perspectives, and actively challenging one's own assumptions and prejudices.

Education and Training: Providing education and training on implicit bias, microaggressions, and cultural competence is essential for raising awareness and promoting inclusive behaviours. Institutions should implement ongoing training programs that encourage continuous learning and growth.

Policy Reforms: Institutions must critically examine their policies and practices to identify and eliminate hidden forms of discrimination. This includes implementing equitable policies, promoting diversity in leadership, and ensuring accountability for discriminatory practices.

Community Engagement: Engaging communities in the process of addressing hidden racism is crucial for developing effective and sustainable solutions. This involves creating spaces for dialogue, involving community members in decision-making processes, and supporting grassroots initiatives.

Promoting Inclusivity: Creating inclusive environments where diversity is genuinely valued involves fostering a culture of respect, support, and empowerment for all individuals. This includes promoting diverse representation, providing support networks, and celebrating the contributions of marginalized communities.

Understanding and addressing hidden racism requires continuous effort and vigilance. As we delve deeper into this topic, we will explore additional aspects of hidden racism, including how it manifests in workplace dynamics, educational settings, and social interactions. This section aims to provide a comprehensive understanding of the subtle ways in which racism can pervade daily life and the strategies needed to combat it.

Workplace Dynamics

Hidden racism in the workplace can significantly impact the career trajectories and job satisfaction of employees of color. While explicit discrimination might be less common, subtle forms of racism often persist, influencing hiring practices, promotion opportunities, and workplace culture.

Hiring Practices: Implicit biases can influence hiring decisions, leading to a preference for candidates who fit the perceived "norm" of the organization. This often means that candidates from minority backgrounds are overlooked in favour of those who are more similar to the existing workforce. Blind recruitment processes, where identifying details such as names and addresses are removed from applications, can help mitigate this bias.

Promotion and Advancement: Employees of color may face additional hurdles in advancing their careers due to hidden racism. This can include being passed over for promotions, receiving less mentorship and support, and having their accomplishments downplayed or ignored. Implementing transparent promotion criteria and mentorship programs that actively support minority employees can help address these disparities.

Workplace Culture: The culture of an organization plays a crucial role in either perpetuating or challenging hidden racism. A workplace that fails to actively promote diversity and inclusion can create an environment where microaggressions and exclusionary practices thrive. Organizations should foster an inclusive culture by promoting diversity training, encouraging open dialogue about race, and celebrating cultural differences.

Educational Settings

Educational institutions are not immune to hidden racism, which can affect students' academic experiences and outcomes. From the curriculum to classroom interactions, hidden racism can influence how students of color are perceived and treated.

Curriculum Bias: The content of school curricula often reflects a Eurocentric perspective, marginalizing the contributions and histories of non-white cultures. This can leave students of color feeling disconnected from their education and undervalued. Curriculum reform that includes diverse perspectives and histories is essential for creating an inclusive educational environment.

Teacher Expectations: Implicit biases held by educators can impact their expectations of students' abilities and behaviour. Research has shown that teachers may have lower expectations for students of color, which can influence student performance and self-esteem. Providing bias training for teachers and encouraging reflective teaching practices can help mitigate these biases.

Disciplinary Actions: Disparities in school discipline are a significant issue, with students of color more likely to face harsher punishments for similar behaviours compared to their white peers. Restorative justice practices, which focus on reconciliation and understanding rather than punishment, can help address these disparities and create a more supportive school environment.

Social Interactions

Hidden racism also permeates social interactions, shaping the ways in which individuals from different racial backgrounds relate to one another. These interactions can reinforce stereotypes and contribute to a climate of exclusion and mistrust.

Social Exclusion: Individuals of color may experience social exclusion in various settings, from social gatherings to professional networking events. This exclusion can be subtle, such as being overlooked in conversations or not being invited to participate in activities. Creating inclusive social environments where everyone feels welcome and valued is crucial for fostering positive relationships.

Stereotyping and Assumptions: Hidden racism often manifests through the reinforcement of racial stereotypes and assumptions. For example, people might assume that an Asian individual is good at math or that a Black person is naturally athletic. While these assumptions may seem benign, they can limit individuals' opportunities and contribute to a narrow understanding of their identities. Challenging and questioning stereotypes is essential for promoting more nuanced and respectful interactions.

Language and Communication: The language used in everyday interactions can also reflect hidden racism. This includes using racially coded language, making "jokes" about race, or using terms that are culturally insensitive. Raising awareness about the impact of language and encouraging respectful communication are important steps in addressing hidden racism.

Strategies for Combating Hidden Racism

Combating hidden racism requires a proactive and multifaceted approach. Here are some strategies that individuals and institutions can implement to address hidden racism:

Awareness and Education: Raising awareness about hidden racism and its impacts is the first step in addressing it. This involves providing education and training on implicit bias, microaggressions, and cultural competence. Workshops, seminars, and online courses can help individuals understand and recognize hidden forms of racism.

Creating Inclusive Environments: Institutions should strive to create environments where diversity is genuinely valued and individuals from all backgrounds feel supported. This includes implementing inclusive policies, promoting diverse representation, and fostering a culture of respect and inclusion.

Encouraging Dialogue: Open and honest dialogue about race and racism is crucial for addressing hidden racism.

This involves creating safe spaces where individuals can share their experiences, ask questions, and learn from one another. Facilitating discussions about race in the workplace, schools, and community organizations can help break down barriers and promote understanding.

Implementing Accountability Measures: Institutions must hold individuals accountable for discriminatory behaviours and practices. This includes establishing clear policies for reporting and addressing incidents of racism, conducting regular assessments of institutional practices, and ensuring that there are consequences for discriminatory actions.

Supporting Marginalized Communities: Providing support for marginalized communities is essential for promoting equity and inclusion. This can include mentorship programs, scholarships, mental health services, and community resources. By actively supporting individuals from marginalized backgrounds, institutions can help to address the systemic barriers they face.

Advocating for Policy Changes: Advocacy for policy changes at the local, national, and institutional levels is crucial for addressing systemic racism. This involves pushing for reforms in areas such as education, criminal justice, healthcare, and housing to ensure that policies promote equity and address historical injustices.

As we continue to examine the pervasive nature of hidden racism, it is crucial to understand how these subtle forms of discrimination affect different aspects of society. By exploring specific examples and case studies, we can better grasp the depth and complexity of hidden racism and identify strategies for creating more inclusive environments.

Case Studies: Hidden Racism in Different Contexts

Higher Education

In higher education, hidden racism can influence admissions processes, campus culture, and academic experiences. Universities and colleges play a crucial role in shaping future leaders and professionals, making it essential to address hidden racism within these institutions.

Admissions Processes: Implicit biases can influence admissions decisions, leading to the underrepresentation of minority students. Admissions committees may unconsciously favour applicants who fit traditional profiles, which often align with white, middle-class norms. Implementing holistic review processes that consider a wider range of experiences and backgrounds can help to mitigate these biases.

Campus Culture: Campus culture can perpetuate hidden racism through exclusive social norms and practices. Minority students may feel marginalized or isolated in predominantly white institutions. Creating inclusive campus environments involves promoting diverse student organizations, hosting cultural events, and ensuring that campus policies support equity and inclusion.

Academic Experiences: Minority students may face microaggressions and biases from peers and faculty, affecting their academic experiences and performance. Providing cultural competence training for faculty and staff, as well as establishing support networks for minority students, can help to create a more inclusive academic environment.

Workplace Inclusion

Hidden racism in the workplace can affect everything from recruitment to daily interactions and career advancement. Understanding and addressing these issues is crucial for creating equitable and supportive work environments.

Recruitment and Hiring: Recruitment practices can perpetuate hidden racism through biased job descriptions, referral programs, and interview processes. Job descriptions that use coded language or emphasize certain cultural norms can discourage minority candidates from applying. Referral programs that rely on existing networks may also perpetuate homogeneity. Implementing structured interview processes and diverse hiring panels can help to reduce bias in recruitment.

Daily Interactions: Microaggressions and exclusionary behaviours in the workplace can create a hostile environment for minority employees. This can include being interrupted in meetings, having their contributions ignored, or being subjected to racial jokes. Encouraging open dialogue about race and providing training on respectful communication can help to address these issues.

Career Advancement: Hidden racism can affect opportunities for career advancement, with minority employees often facing additional barriers to promotion. This can include lack of mentorship, biased performance evaluations, and exclusion from key projects. Organizations should implement mentorship programs, transparent promotion criteria, and regular diversity audits to ensure equitable opportunities for all employees.

Healthcare Settings

In healthcare settings, hidden racism can lead to disparities in treatment, patient outcomes, and healthcare access. Addressing these issues is vital for promoting health equity and improving the quality of care for all patients.

Treatment Disparities: Implicit biases among healthcare providers can lead to differential treatment for minority patients. For example, studies have shown that Black patients are less likely to receive pain medication compared to white patients with similar conditions. Providing implicit bias training for healthcare providers and implementing standardized treatment protocols can help to reduce these disparities.

Patient Outcomes: Hidden racism can contribute to poorer health outcomes for minority patients. This can include higher rates of chronic illnesses, lower life expectancy, and increased mortality rates. Addressing social determinants of health, such as access to healthy food, safe housing, and quality education, is essential for improving health outcomes.

Healthcare Access: Minority communities often face barriers to accessing healthcare, including lack of insurance, transportation, and culturally competent care. Expanding access to affordable healthcare and increasing the availability of community health centers can help to address these barriers.

Legal and Criminal Justice Systems

Hidden racism in the legal and criminal justice systems can lead to unequal treatment, sentencing disparities, and mistrust between minority communities and law enforcement.

Policing Practices: Implicit biases can influence policing practices, leading to disproportionate targeting of minority communities. This can result in higher arrest rates and increased likelihood of police violence. Implementing bias training for officers, promoting community policing initiatives, and increasing transparency and accountability in law enforcement are essential for addressing these issues.

Sentencing Disparities: Racial disparities in sentencing can result in harsher penalties for minority defendants compared to their white counterparts. This can perpetuate cycles of poverty and incarceration in minority communities. Sentencing reform, including the elimination of mandatory minimum sentences and the implementation of restorative justice practices, is crucial for addressing these disparities.

Trust in the Legal System: Hidden racism can erode trust between minority communities and the legal system. This mistrust can deter individuals from seeking legal assistance or cooperating with law enforcement. Building trust requires addressing systemic biases, promoting diverse representation within the legal profession, and ensuring that legal services are accessible and culturally competent.

Strategies for Combating Hidden Racism

Combating hidden racism requires a comprehensive and sustained effort across multiple sectors of society. Key strategies include:

Education and Awareness: Raising awareness about hidden racism and its impacts is the first step in addressing it. This involves providing education and training on implicit bias, microaggressions, and cultural competence. Workshops, seminars, and online courses can help individuals understand and recognize hidden forms of racism.

Policy and Practice Reforms: Institutions must critically examine their policies and practices to identify and eliminate hidden forms of discrimination. This includes implementing equitable policies, promoting diversity in leadership, and ensuring accountability for discriminatory practices.

Promoting Inclusive Environments: Creating inclusive environments involves fostering a culture of respect, support, and empowerment for all individuals. This includes promoting diverse representation, providing support networks, and celebrating the contributions of marginalized communities.

Encouraging Open Dialogue: Open and honest dialogue about race and racism is crucial for addressing hidden racism. This involves creating safe spaces where individuals can share their experiences, ask questions, and learn from one another. Facilitating discussions about race in the workplace, schools, and community organizations can help break down barriers and promote understanding.

Supporting Marginalized Communities: Providing support for marginalized communities is essential for promoting equity and inclusion. This can include mentorship programs, scholarships, mental health services, and community resources. By actively supporting individuals from marginalized backgrounds, institutions can help to address the systemic barriers they face.

Advocacy and Activism: Advocacy and activism play a critical role in pushing for policy changes and holding institutions accountable. Supporting organizations and movements that advocate for racial justice and creating opportunities for collective action can help to drive systemic change.

In our exploration of hidden racism, it is essential to recognize the pervasive impact it has on various sectors of society and the importance of addressing it comprehensively. This final section of the chapter delves into additional contexts where hidden racism manifests, including media, technology, and mental health, and discusses strategies to combat these subtle forms of discrimination.

Media and Representation

The media plays a significant role in shaping public perceptions and cultural norms. Hidden racism in media can perpetuate stereotypes, reinforce biases, and marginalize minority voices.

Stereotypical Portrayals: Media often relies on stereotypical portrayals of racial and ethnic minorities, which can reinforce harmful biases. For example, Black individuals might be frequently depicted as criminals, Latinos as illegal immigrants, or Asians as the "model minority." These portrayals can influence public perceptions and contribute to a narrow understanding of these communities.

Underrepresentation: Minority groups are often underrepresented in media, both in front of and behind the camera. This lack of representation can lead to a limited range of stories and perspectives being told, further marginalizing these communities. Efforts to promote diversity in media production and content are crucial for ensuring that a wider array of voices and experiences are represented.

Media Literacy: Promoting media literacy is essential for helping individuals recognize and critically assess hidden racism in media. Education programs that teach people to analyze media content, understand its impact, and challenge stereotypes can empower audiences to demand more accurate and inclusive representation.

Technology and Algorithmic Bias

As technology becomes increasingly integrated into our lives, it is essential to recognize and address hidden racism within this sphere. Algorithmic bias and discrimination in technology can have significant implications for equity and inclusion.

Algorithmic Bias: Algorithms used in various applications, from hiring platforms to law enforcement tools, can perpetuate hidden racism if they are based on biased data or flawed assumptions. For example, facial recognition technology has been shown to have higher error rates for people of color, leading to potential misidentifications and discriminatory practices.

Discrimination in Tech: The tech industry itself can be a breeding ground for hidden racism, with disparities in hiring, promotion, and workplace culture. Minority tech professionals often face barriers to entry and advancement, as well as a lack of support and representation.

Ethical AI Development: Addressing hidden racism in technology requires a commitment to ethical AI development and the inclusion of diverse perspectives in the design and implementation of tech solutions. This involves conducting thorough bias audits, diversifying tech teams, and creating accountability frameworks for technology companies.

Mental Health and Well-Being

Hidden racism can have profound effects on the mental health and well-being of individuals from marginalized communities. The cumulative impact of subtle discrimination, microaggressions, and systemic barriers can contribute to psychological stress and trauma.

Mental Health Disparities: Minority populations often face disparities in access to mental health care, as well as in the quality of care they receive. Cultural stigma, lack of culturally competent providers, and economic barriers can all contribute to these disparities.

Psychological Impact: The psychological impact of hidden racism includes increased stress, anxiety, depression, and feelings of isolation. These effects can be exacerbated by the ongoing need to navigate and cope with subtle forms of discrimination in daily life.

Culturally Competent Care: Providing culturally competent mental health care is essential for addressing the unique needs of minority populations. This includes training mental health professionals to understand and address the impact of racism, as well as increasing access to mental health services in marginalized communities.

Strategies for Combating Hidden Racism

Promoting Diversity and Inclusion: Promoting diversity and inclusion across all sectors of society is crucial for addressing hidden racism. This involves implementing policies and practices that support the representation and empowerment of minority groups, creating inclusive environments, and actively challenging discriminatory behaviours.

Community Engagement and Advocacy: Engaging with communities and supporting grassroots advocacy efforts are essential for driving systemic change. This includes creating spaces for dialogue, involving community members in decision-making processes, and supporting initiatives that promote racial equity and justice.

Policy Reforms and Accountability: Policy reforms that address systemic barriers and promote equity are critical for combating hidden racism. Institutions must implement accountability measures to ensure that policies are effectively addressing disparities and promoting inclusion.

Education and Awareness: Raising awareness about hidden racism and its impact is vital for fostering a more inclusive society. Education programs, training workshops, and public awareness campaigns can help individuals recognize and challenge their own biases, as well as advocate for broader societal change.

Support Networks and Resources: Providing support networks and resources for individuals affected by hidden racism is crucial for promoting resilience and well-being. This includes mentorship programs, mental health services, and community support groups that offer guidance and solidarity.

Hidden racism is a pervasive and insidious form of discrimination that affects various aspects of society. By understanding how hidden racism manifests in media, technology, mental health, and other contexts, we can develop comprehensive strategies to address these subtle forms of discrimination. Combating hidden racism requires collective effort, commitment, and a willingness to confront uncomfortable truths in order to create a more just and inclusive world.

In the next chapter, we will explore the impact of racism on different cultures, examining how racial discrimination affects various ethnic groups and the ways in which these communities have resisted and responded to racism. By understanding the diverse experiences of racial discrimination, we can better appreciate the complexity of racism and the importance of promoting equity and inclusion.

Chapter 10: The Impact of Racism on Different Cultures

Racism affects cultures in profound and varied ways, influencing everything from language and traditions to economic opportunities and social dynamics. This chapter examines the cultural impact of racism on various ethnic groups, highlighting both the damage done and the resilience shown by these communities. Understanding these diverse experiences is crucial for appreciating the complexity of racism and promoting equity and inclusion.

The African American Experience

The African American experience with racism is deeply rooted in the history of slavery, segregation, and ongoing systemic discrimination in the United States. This history has shaped African American culture in unique and significant ways.

Cultural Contributions: Despite the pervasive racism they have faced, African Americans have made profound contributions to American culture. From music genres like jazz, blues, and hip-hop to literature, art, and fashion, African American cultural expressions have had a lasting impact on American and global culture. These contributions have often served as a form of resistance and resilience, highlighting the creativity and strength of the African American community.

Economic Disparities: Systemic racism has led to significant economic disparities between African Americans and their white counterparts. Issues such as the racial wealth gap, unequal access to education, and discriminatory housing practices have limited economic opportunities for African Americans. Efforts to address these disparities include advocating for reparations, economic empowerment programs, and policy reforms aimed at promoting equity.

Social and Political Activism: African Americans have been at the forefront of social and political activism, advocating for civil rights and racial justice. Movements like the Civil Rights Movement of the 1950s and 1960s and the more recent Black Lives Matter movement have brought attention to issues of racial injustice and pushed for systemic change. This activism has been instrumental in securing legal and social advancements for African Americans and other marginalized groups.

The Latinx Experience

The Latinx community in the United States is diverse, encompassing people from various Latin American countries and cultural backgrounds. Racism and discrimination have significantly impacted Latinx individuals and communities, influencing their cultural identity and social experiences.

Cultural Identity: Latinx individuals often navigate complex cultural identities, balancing their heritage with the pressures to assimilate into mainstream American culture. This dual identity can be both a source of strength and a challenge, as Latinx individuals strive to preserve their cultural traditions while also seeking acceptance in a society that often marginalizes them.

Immigration and Xenophobia: The Latinx community has been significantly affected by immigration policies and xenophobia. Anti-immigrant rhetoric and discriminatory policies have led to increased scrutiny and marginalization of Latinx individuals, particularly those who are undocumented. Advocacy for immigrant rights and comprehensive immigration reform is crucial for addressing these issues and promoting the inclusion of Latinx individuals in American society.

Educational and Economic Barriers: Latinx individuals often face barriers to education and economic opportunities. Issues such as language barriers, underfunded schools in predominantly Latinx neighborhoods, and discriminatory hiring practices can limit opportunities for social mobility. Efforts to address these barriers include bilingual education programs, mentorship initiatives, and policies aimed at promoting diversity and inclusion in the workplace.

The Asian American Experience

The Asian American experience with racism is characterized by a history of exclusion, stereotyping, and systemic discrimination. Despite these challenges, Asian Americans have made significant contributions to American culture and society.

Stereotypes and Model Minority Myth: Asian Americans often contend with stereotypes and the "model minority" myth, which portrays them as successful and hardworking but also as perpetual foreigners. This myth can mask the diversity of experiences within the Asian American community and obscure the challenges they face, such as economic disparities and discrimination.

Historical Exclusion: Asian Americans have a history of exclusion, exemplified by policies such as the Chinese Exclusion Act of 1882 and the internment of Japanese Americans during World War II. These policies have left a lasting impact on the community, contributing to feelings of marginalization and mistrust of governmental institutions.

Community Resilience: Despite these challenges, Asian Americans have demonstrated remarkable resilience and have made significant contributions to American society. From innovations in technology and science to achievements in the arts and entertainment, Asian Americans continue to shape and enrich American culture. Advocacy for Asian American rights and visibility has also grown, particularly in response to recent increases in anti-Asian hate crimes and discrimination.

The Indigenous Experience

Indigenous peoples in the United States have faced centuries of colonization, displacement, and systemic racism. These experiences have profoundly impacted their cultural practices, social structures, and overall well-being.

Cultural Preservation: Indigenous communities have worked tirelessly to preserve their cultural traditions, languages, and practices in the face of ongoing marginalization. Efforts to revitalize Indigenous languages, reclaim cultural practices, and promote traditional knowledge are essential for maintaining Indigenous identity and heritage.

Land Rights and Sovereignty: Issues of land rights and sovereignty are central to the Indigenous experience. The loss of ancestral lands and the infringement on tribal sovereignty have had devastating effects on Indigenous communities. Advocacy for the protection of land rights, recognition of sovereignty, and environmental justice are critical components of the broader struggle for Indigenous rights.

Health Disparities: Indigenous peoples often face significant health disparities, including higher rates of chronic illnesses, mental health issues, and limited access to healthcare services. Addressing these disparities requires a holistic approach that includes culturally competent healthcare, investment in community health initiatives, and policies that address the social determinants of health.

 The African Diaspora in Europe

The African diaspora in Europe, including individuals of African, Caribbean, and Afro-Latinx descent, faces unique challenges related to racism and discrimination. The historical and contemporary experiences of these communities vary across countries, but common themes include marginalization, economic disparities, and cultural resilience.

Historical Legacies: The legacy of colonialism and the transatlantic slave trade continues to shape the experiences of the African diaspora in Europe. This history has contributed to systemic racism and the marginalization of Black communities in various European countries.

Economic Inequality: Economic inequality is a significant issue for the African diaspora in Europe. Discrimination in employment, housing, and education can limit opportunities for social mobility and economic advancement. Efforts to address these disparities include advocating for anti-discrimination policies, promoting diversity in hiring practices, and supporting economic empowerment initiatives.

Cultural Expression: Despite the challenges they face, individuals of the African diaspora in Europe have made significant cultural contributions, enriching European societies with diverse traditions, music, art, and literature. Cultural expression has often served as a form of resistance and empowerment, highlighting the resilience and creativity of these communities.

The Middle Eastern and North African Experience

Individuals from the Middle East and North Africa (MENA) region face distinct forms of racism and discrimination, often influenced by geopolitical factors, cultural stereotypes, and Islamophobia.

Stereotypes and Islamophobia: Stereotypes about individuals from the MENA region often intersect with Islamophobia, leading to discrimination and marginalization. The portrayal of Middle Eastern and North African individuals as terrorists or extremists in media and political discourse contributes to a climate of fear and suspicion.

Immigration and Refugee Status: Many individuals from the MENA region have sought refuge in other countries due to conflict and instability in their home countries. The experience of being an immigrant or refugee can involve navigating significant barriers to integration, including language barriers, economic challenges, and cultural adjustment.

Cultural Resilience: Despite facing significant challenges, individuals from the MENA region have shown remarkable resilience and have enriched their host countries with their cultural contributions. Efforts to combat Islamophobia and promote understanding and inclusion are crucial for supporting the integration and well-being of these communities.

As we continue exploring the impact of racism on different cultures, it is essential to understand how racial discrimination affects not only individual communities but also broader societal dynamics. This section delves into additional ethnic groups and their experiences with racism, highlighting the resilience, resistance, and cultural contributions of these communities.

The Jewish Experience

The Jewish community has faced centuries of persecution and discrimination, culminating in the Holocaust during World War II. Despite these historical traumas, Jewish culture has demonstrated remarkable resilience and has made significant contributions to society.

Historical Persecution: Anti-Semitism, the prejudice against Jews, has been a persistent issue throughout history. From medieval pogroms to the horrors of the Holocaust, Jews have faced systemic violence and discrimination. This history has shaped Jewish identity and community cohesion, fostering a strong sense of solidarity and mutual support.

Cultural Contributions: Jewish culture has enriched global society in numerous ways, from contributions in science, literature, and art to advancements in philosophy and medicine. Jewish thinkers like Albert Einstein, Sigmund Freud, and Hannah Arendt have had profound impacts on their respective fields, showcasing the intellectual and cultural vibrancy of the Jewish community.

Contemporary Anti-Semitism: Despite progress in many areas, anti-Semitism remains a significant issue. Hate crimes against Jews, including vandalism of synagogues and violent attacks, continue to occur. Addressing contemporary anti-Semitism requires ongoing vigilance, education, and the promotion of interfaith dialogue to foster understanding and respect.

The Romani Experience

The Romani people, often referred to as "Gypsies," have faced long-standing prejudice and discrimination across Europe. Their experiences highlight the deep-seated racism and exclusion that persist against nomadic and marginalized communities.

Historical Marginalization: The Romani people have been subjected to systemic exclusion and persecution for centuries. During the Holocaust, hundreds of thousands of Romani were killed in concentration camps. This history of marginalization has had lasting effects on

Romani communities, including economic and social disenfranchisement.

Cultural Richness: Despite the challenges they face, the Romani people have a rich cultural heritage characterized by vibrant music, dance, and storytelling traditions. These cultural expressions serve as a means of preserving Romani identity and resisting assimilation pressures.

Contemporary Discrimination: Today, the Romani continue to face discrimination in education, employment, and housing. They are often depicted negatively in media, perpetuating harmful stereotypes. Efforts to combat discrimination against the Romani include advocacy for equal rights, inclusive policies, and initiatives that celebrate Romani culture.

The Indigenous Peoples of Australia

The Aboriginal and Torres Strait Islander peoples of Australia have endured significant discrimination and marginalization since the arrival of European settlers. Their experiences underscore the ongoing struggle for recognition, rights, and reconciliation.

Colonial Impact: The colonization of Australia led to the dispossession of Indigenous lands, the destruction of traditional ways of life, and widespread violence against Indigenous peoples. Policies such as the forced removal of children, known as the Stolen Generations, aimed to assimilate Indigenous peoples into white society, causing lasting trauma and disruption to communities.

Cultural Revival: In response to these historical injustices, there has been a strong movement towards cultural revival and reclamation of Indigenous identity. Efforts to preserve and promote Indigenous languages, arts, and traditions are central to this movement, fostering a sense of pride and resilience among Aboriginal and Torres Strait Islander peoples.

Reconciliation Efforts: Reconciliation initiatives in Australia aim to address past wrongs and build a more inclusive society. These efforts include formal apologies from the government, such as the National Apology to the Stolen Generations, and programs designed to improve health, education, and economic outcomes for Indigenous communities. True reconciliation requires ongoing commitment and collaboration between Indigenous and non-Indigenous Australians.

The Experience of Afro-Latinx Communities

Afro-Latinx communities, comprising individuals of African descent in Latin America and the Caribbean, face unique challenges related to racism and discrimination. Their experiences highlight the intersectionality of race and ethnicity in shaping social dynamics.

Historical Context: The legacy of the transatlantic slave trade and colonialism has profoundly influenced the experiences of Afro-Latinx communities. Enslaved Africans were brought to Latin America and the Caribbean to work on plantations, and their descendants continue to face systemic racism and social exclusion.

Cultural Resilience: Afro-Latinx culture is characterized by a rich blend of African, Indigenous, and European influences. From music genres like salsa, reggae, and samba to vibrant religious practices such as Candomblé and Santería, Afro-Latinx cultural expressions reflect the resilience and creativity of these communities.

Social and Economic Disparities: Afro-Latinx individuals often face significant social and economic disparities, including higher rates of poverty, limited access to education, and discrimination in the labour market. Addressing these disparities requires targeted policies and programs that promote equity and inclusion.

The Impact on Refugee and Immigrant Communities

Refugee and immigrant communities from diverse backgrounds face unique challenges related to racism and xenophobia. Their experiences underscore the need for inclusive policies and practices that support integration and respect for cultural diversity.

Refugee Experiences: Refugees fleeing conflict, persecution, and economic instability often encounter racism and xenophobia in their host countries. This can include discrimination in housing, employment, and access to services. Efforts to support refugees should focus on providing comprehensive integration programs, legal protections, and community support networks.

Immigrant Integration: Immigrant communities contribute significantly to the social and economic fabric of their host countries. However, they may also face challenges related to language barriers, cultural adjustment, and discrimination. Policies that promote language acquisition, cultural competence, and equal opportunities are essential for successful integration.

Celebrating Diversity: Embracing cultural diversity involves recognizing and valuing the contributions of immigrant and refugee communities. Celebrating cultural festivals, promoting multicultural education, and fostering inclusive public spaces can help to create a more welcoming and cohesive society.

Strategies for Supporting Diverse Communities

Supporting diverse communities and addressing the impact of racism requires a multifaceted approach that includes policy reforms, community engagement, and cultural celebration.

Policy Reforms: Implementing policies that promote equity and inclusion is essential for addressing systemic barriers faced by marginalized communities. This includes anti-discrimination laws, affirmative action programs, and policies that support economic empowerment and social mobility.

Community Engagement: Engaging with communities to understand their unique needs and challenges is crucial for developing effective solutions. This involves creating platforms for dialogue, supporting grassroots initiatives, and involving community members in decision-making processes.

Cultural Celebration: Celebrating the cultural contributions of diverse communities fosters a sense of belonging and mutual respect. This can include supporting cultural festivals, promoting arts and heritage programs, and integrating diverse perspectives into educational curricula.

Education and Awareness: Raising awareness about the experiences and contributions of marginalized communities is vital for promoting understanding and empathy. Education programs, public awareness campaigns, and media representation play key roles in challenging stereotypes and fostering inclusivity.

Racism affects cultures in profound and varied ways, influencing everything from economic opportunities to social dynamics and cultural expression. By examining the experiences of different ethnic groups, we gain a deeper understanding of the complexity of racism and the importance of promoting equity and inclusion. The resilience and contributions of marginalized communities highlight the strength and creativity that arise in the face of adversity.

In the next chapter, we will explore the idea that not everyone is racist or bad, emphasizing the complexities of human behaviour and the capacity for change and growth. By acknowledging the positive efforts of allies and advocates, we can build a more inclusive and supportive society.

Chapter 11: Not Everyone Is Racist or Bad

While it is crucial to acknowledge and address the pervasive nature of racism, it is equally important to recognize that not everyone holds racist beliefs or engages in discriminatory behaviour. Understanding the complexities of human behaviour and the capacity for change and growth allows us to see the potential for positive efforts toward racial equality. This chapter emphasizes the positive contributions of allies and advocates, highlighting the importance of empathy, education, and collective action in building a more inclusive and supportive society.

The Role of Allies

Allies are individuals who support marginalized groups and actively work to promote equality and justice. Allies play a crucial role in challenging racism and advocating for change. Their efforts can significantly impact the fight against racism and contribute to a more inclusive society.

Educating Themselves: Effective allies begin by educating themselves about the history and realities of racism. This involves reading books, attending workshops, and engaging with resources created by marginalized communities. By gaining a deeper understanding of the issues, allies can better support and advocate for racial justice.

Listening and Amplifying Voices: Allies must listen to the experiences and perspectives of marginalized individuals. This means creating space for these voices to be heard and amplifying their messages rather than speaking over them. Listening with empathy and validating the experiences of people of color are essential steps in supporting their fight for justice.

Taking Action: Allies should not only educate themselves and listen but also take concrete actions to combat racism. This can include participating in protests, supporting anti-racist organizations, and using their platforms to raise awareness. Allies can also work within their own communities to challenge racist behaviours and advocate for inclusive policies.

Empathy and Understanding

Empathy and understanding are fundamental to addressing racism and building inclusive communities. By developing a deeper sense of empathy, individuals can connect with the experiences of others and foster a culture of respect and solidarity.

Personal Connections: Personal connections and relationships with individuals from different racial and ethnic backgrounds can help to break down prejudices and stereotypes. These relationships provide opportunities for meaningful dialogue and mutual understanding.

Storytelling and Media: Storytelling and media play a powerful role in fostering empathy. Films, books, and other forms of media that portray the experiences of marginalized communities can help individuals understand the impact of racism on a personal level. These narratives can challenge existing biases and promote a more inclusive worldview.

Education and Dialogue: Education and open dialogue about race and racism are crucial for fostering empathy and understanding. This includes integrating diverse perspectives into educational curricula, hosting community discussions, and creating safe spaces for conversations about race. By encouraging open and honest dialogue, communities can work towards greater understanding and solidarity.

The Capacity for Change

Human behaviour is complex, and individuals have the capacity for growth and change. Acknowledging this potential allows us to see the possibilities for progress and transformation in the fight against racism.

Challenging Biases: Individuals can challenge and change their own biases through self-reflection and education. Recognizing and addressing implicit biases is an ongoing process that requires commitment and effort. By becoming aware of their own prejudices, individuals can work towards more equitable and inclusive behaviours.

Learning from Mistakes: Everyone makes mistakes, but it is how we respond to those mistakes that matters. Acknowledging and learning from past behaviours and actions that may have been harmful is an important step in personal growth. This involves taking responsibility, apologizing when necessary, and making a conscious effort to change.

Supporting Positive Change: Encouraging and supporting positive change in others is also crucial. This includes creating environments where individuals feel safe to discuss their biases and learn from their mistakes. By fostering a culture of growth and support, we can promote collective progress towards racial equality.

The Impact of Advocacy

Advocacy efforts by individuals and organizations have played a significant role in advancing racial justice. These efforts demonstrate the power of collective action and the importance of standing in solidarity with marginalized communities.

Civil Rights Movement: The Civil Rights Movement of the 1950s and 1960s is a powerful example of how collective action can bring about significant social change. Leaders like Martin Luther King Jr., Rosa Parks, and many others mobilized communities to challenge segregation and fight for equal rights. Their efforts led to landmark legislation, such as the Civil Rights Act of 1964 and the Voting Rights Act of 1965.

Modern-Day Movements: Contemporary movements like Black Lives Matter continue to advocate for racial justice and equality. These movements highlight the ongoing issues of police brutality, systemic racism, and social inequality. By mobilizing communities and raising awareness, these movements push for policy changes and greater accountability.

Grassroots Organizations: Grassroots organizations play a vital role in advocating for racial justice at the local level. These organizations often address specific issues within their communities, such as education equity, housing discrimination, and healthcare access. Their work is essential for creating sustainable change and supporting marginalized individuals.

Building Inclusive Communities

Building inclusive communities requires collective effort and a commitment to promoting equity and justice. By working together, individuals and organizations can create environments where everyone feels valued and respected.

Inclusive Policies and Practices: Implementing inclusive policies and practices is essential for promoting equity. This includes anti-discrimination policies, diversity and inclusion initiatives, and equitable resource allocation. Institutions should regularly assess and revise their policies to ensure they are effectively addressing disparities.

Community Engagement: Engaging with communities to understand their needs and challenges is crucial for developing effective solutions. This involves creating platforms for dialogue, supporting community-led initiatives, and involving community members in decision-making processes.

Celebrating Diversity: Celebrating diversity involves recognizing and valuing the contributions of all individuals. This can include supporting cultural festivals, promoting diverse representation in media and leadership, and integrating diverse perspectives into educational curricula.

Continuing to explore the complexities of human behaviour and the capacity for change, this section delves into additional examples of positive efforts and the importance of fostering an inclusive and supportive society. Recognizing the good in people and their potential for growth can help us build stronger, more united communities.

The Role of Institutions

Institutions, from educational establishments to corporations, play a pivotal role in shaping societal attitudes and behaviours. When these institutions commit to promoting diversity, equity, and inclusion, they can significantly impact the fight against racism.

Educational Institutions: Schools and universities have the power to influence future generations. By implementing comprehensive diversity and inclusion programs, these institutions can educate students about the importance of racial equality and provide them with the tools to challenge discrimination. Initiatives such as inclusive curricula, diversity training for staff, and support networks for marginalized students are essential for creating a more equitable educational environment.

Corporate Responsibility: Corporations also have a significant role in promoting racial justice. Many companies are now recognizing the importance of diversity in the workplace and are taking steps to create more inclusive environments. This includes implementing bias training, establishing diversity councils, and setting measurable diversity goals. By prioritizing diversity and inclusion, corporations can contribute to broader societal change.

Non-Profit Organizations: Non-profit organizations dedicated to racial justice and equality are crucial in advocating for change and supporting marginalized communities. These organizations often provide essential services, such as legal assistance, educational programs, and advocacy work. Supporting and collaborating with non-profits can amplify efforts to combat racism and promote inclusion.

Community Initiatives

Grassroots community initiatives are often the driving force behind meaningful change. These initiatives, led by community members, address specific local issues and work towards creating inclusive and supportive environments.

Local Advocacy Groups: Local advocacy groups focus on addressing issues of racism and discrimination within their communities. These groups often organize events, workshops, and campaigns to raise awareness and promote racial justice. By mobilizing community members and fostering solidarity, local advocacy groups can create significant change at the grassroots level.

Cultural and Community Centers: Cultural and community centers play a vital role in supporting marginalized communities and promoting cultural exchange. These centers provide a space for individuals to celebrate their heritage, access resources, and engage in community-building activities. By fostering a sense of belonging and mutual respect, cultural and community centers contribute to the creation of inclusive communities.

Youth Programs: Youth programs that focus on leadership development, education, and social justice are essential for empowering the next generation of advocates. These programs provide young people with the skills and knowledge to challenge racism and promote equity. By investing in youth, communities can ensure that the fight for racial justice continues into the future.

 Individual Efforts

While collective action is crucial, individual efforts to combat racism and promote inclusion are equally important. Each person has the power to make a difference through their actions and choices.

Self-Reflection and Education: Individuals can start by reflecting on their own biases and educating themselves about racism and its impacts. This involves seeking out resources, engaging in conversations, and being open to feedback. Continuous self-education is essential for personal growth and effective allyship.

Challenging Racism: Speaking out against racist behaviours and attitudes, whether in the workplace, social settings, or online, is a critical aspect of individual action. By challenging racism when it occurs, individuals can help create environments where discriminatory behaviour is not tolerated.

Supporting Marginalized Communities: Supporting marginalized communities involves both advocacy and direct action. This can include volunteering with organizations that work towards racial justice, donating to causes that support marginalized individuals, and using one's platform to amplify marginalized voices. Every small action contributes to the broader movement for equity and inclusion.

The Power of Empathy and Compassion

Empathy and compassion are powerful tools in the fight against racism. By understanding and sharing the feelings of others, individuals can build stronger, more supportive communities.

Active Listening: Active listening involves fully concentrating, understanding, responding, and remembering what is being said. By truly listening to the experiences of marginalized individuals, people can develop a deeper understanding of the impact of racism and the importance of advocating for change.

Building Relationships: Building genuine relationships across racial and ethnic lines can help break down prejudices and foster mutual respect. These relationships provide opportunities for meaningful dialogue and collaboration, contributing to a more inclusive society.

Practicing Compassion: Practicing compassion means being sensitive to the suffering of others and being motivated to help alleviate it. Acts of kindness and support, whether big or small, can make a significant difference in the lives of those affected by racism.

Success Stories

Highlighting success stories of individuals and communities that have effectively combated racism and promoted inclusion can inspire others to act.

Educational Reform: Schools that have successfully implemented inclusive curricula and diversity training can serve as models for other institutions. These schools demonstrate how education can be a powerful tool for promoting equity and understanding.

Corporate Initiatives: Companies that have made significant strides in diversity and inclusion, such as through comprehensive diversity programs and equitable hiring practices, can inspire other organizations to follow suit. These companies show that prioritizing diversity is not only the right thing to do but also beneficial for business.

Community Movements: Grassroots movements that have successfully addressed local issues of racism and discrimination provide valuable lessons in advocacy and community organizing. These movements illustrate the power of collective action and the importance of community-driven solutions.

Not everyone is racist or bad, and many individuals actively work to combat racism and promote equity and inclusion. By recognizing the positive contributions of allies and advocates, we can build a more inclusive and supportive society. Empathy, understanding, and a commitment to personal and collective growth are essential for fostering positive change. The capacity for change and the impact of advocacy efforts highlights the potential for progress in the fight against racism.

In the next chapter, we will explore whether things are getting better, assessing the progress made in advancing racial equality and identifying the areas where work still needs to be done. By evaluating the current state of racial justice, we can better understand the challenges and opportunities that lie ahead.

Chapter 12: Are Things Getting Better?

Assessing whether things are getting better in the fight against racism involves examining the progress made over recent decades, identifying the areas where significant strides have been taken, and recognizing the challenges that remain. This chapter provides an overview of the advancements in racial equality, evaluates current disparities, and explores the ongoing efforts needed to achieve true equity.

Historical Progress

The fight against racism has seen significant progress over the past century, with numerous legal, social, and cultural advancements contributing to greater racial equality.

Legal Reforms: Landmark legal reforms have been instrumental in challenging institutional racism and promoting civil rights. In the United States, the Civil Rights Act of 1964 and the Voting Rights Act of 1965 were pivotal in dismantling segregation and protecting the voting rights of Black Americans. Similar anti-discrimination laws have been enacted in other countries, contributing to the global fight against racism.

Social Movements: Social movements have played a crucial role in advancing racial equality. The Civil Rights Movement, led by figures such as Martin Luther King Jr. and Rosa Parks, brought national and international attention to the plight of African Americans and inspired subsequent movements for racial justice. More recently, movements like Black Lives Matter have highlighted ongoing issues of police brutality and systemic racism, mobilizing millions around the world.

Educational Improvements: There has been a significant increase in access to education for marginalized communities. Efforts to desegregate schools, provide scholarships, and implement affirmative action policies have contributed to greater educational opportunities for students of color. Higher education institutions are also increasingly incorporating diverse perspectives into their curricula.

Current Disparities

Despite the progress made, significant racial disparities persist across various sectors, indicating that much work remains to be done to achieve true equity.

Economic Inequality: Racial wealth gaps continue to be a significant issue, with people of color, particularly Black and Latino communities, experiencing higher rates of poverty and unemployment compared to their white counterparts. Discriminatory lending practices, unequal access to capital, and historical injustices such as redlining have contributed to these disparities.

Healthcare Disparities: Minority communities often face disparities in health outcomes, including higher rates of chronic illnesses and lower life expectancy. Factors contributing to these disparities include limited access to healthcare, implicit biases among healthcare providers, and socioeconomic determinants of health.

Criminal Justice System: Racial disparities in the criminal justice system remain a critical concern. Black and Latino individuals are disproportionately affected by mass incarceration, police violence, and harsher sentencing practices. These disparities highlight the need for comprehensive criminal justice reform to address systemic biases.

Educational Gaps: While access to education has improved, significant gaps in academic achievement and resources persist. Schools in predominantly minority neighborhoods often lack adequate funding, experienced teachers, and essential resources, contributing to lower educational outcomes for students of color.

Ongoing Efforts

Efforts to address these disparities and promote racial equality are ongoing and multifaceted, involving policy reforms, community initiatives, and advocacy.

Policy Reforms: Governments and institutions are implementing policy reforms to address systemic racism. This includes initiatives to promote economic equity, such as reparations, affordable housing programs, and job training initiatives. Healthcare policies aimed at reducing disparities and improving access to care for marginalized communities are also being pursued.

Community Initiatives: Grassroots organizations and community initiatives continue to play a vital role in advocating for racial justice and supporting marginalized communities. These initiatives often focus on specific local issues, providing direct support and resources to those in need.

Educational Programs: Educational programs that promote cultural competence, diversity, and inclusion are essential for fostering understanding and empathy. Schools and universities are increasingly adopting curricula that reflect the diverse experiences and contributions of all racial and ethnic groups.

Advocacy and Activism: Advocacy and activism remain crucial in pushing for systemic change. Organizations and movements dedicated to racial justice continue to raise awareness, mobilize communities, and advocate for policy changes. By amplifying marginalized voices and highlighting ongoing injustices, these efforts keep the fight for racial equality at the forefront of public consciousness.

Evaluating Progress

To evaluate whether things are truly getting better, it is essential to consider both quantitative and qualitative measures of progress.

Quantitative Measures: Quantitative measures include statistical data on economic, educational, health, and criminal justice disparities. While some indicators show improvement, such as increased educational attainment and decreased poverty rates among certain minority groups, others highlight persistent inequalities that need to be addressed.

Qualitative Measures: Qualitative measures involve assessing the lived experiences of marginalized individuals and communities. This includes understanding how people of color perceive their treatment in various sectors, their sense of belonging and inclusion, and their overall quality of life. Surveys, interviews, and focus groups can provide valuable insights into these experiences.

Intersectional Analysis: An intersectional analysis considers how different aspects of identity, such as race, gender, class, and sexuality, intersect to create unique experiences of discrimination and privilege. Evaluating progress through an intersectional lens helps to identify specific challenges faced by individuals at the intersection of multiple marginalized identities and to develop targeted strategies for addressing these challenges.

Global Perspective

Racism is a global issue, and evaluating progress requires a global perspective. Different countries have made varying degrees of progress in addressing racism, influenced by their unique historical, social, and political contexts.

Progress in Europe: European countries have made strides in addressing racism through anti-discrimination laws, diversity initiatives, and social movements. However, issues such as xenophobia, Islamophobia, and discrimination against Romani and African communities remain significant challenges.

Challenges in Latin America: In Latin America, racial discrimination often intersects with issues of economic inequality and indigenous rights. Efforts to address these challenges include constitutional reforms, affirmative action policies, and indigenous movements advocating for land rights and cultural preservation.

Advancements in Africa: African countries continue to address the legacy of colonialism and apartheid. Efforts include promoting economic development, protecting human rights, and fostering political stability. Regional organizations, such as the African Union, play a crucial role in advancing these goals.

Media Representation and Influence

The media has a powerful influence on societal attitudes and perceptions. Positive changes in media representation and coverage have contributed to raising awareness about racism and promoting more inclusive narratives.

Positive Representation: Over the past few decades, there has been an increase in the positive representation of people of color in films, television shows, and advertisements. Shows like Black-ish, Pose, and Master of None have highlighted diverse experiences and stories, challenging stereotypes and promoting a more nuanced understanding of different racial and ethnic groups. This shift in representation helps to normalize diversity and fosters empathy and understanding.

Diverse Storytelling: The rise of diverse storytellers in the media industry has led to a broader range of perspectives and experiences being shared. Directors, writers, and producers from marginalized communities are creating content that reflects their realities and challenges dominant narratives. By amplifying these voices, the media can play a crucial role in combating racism and promoting inclusivity.

Media Accountability: Media organizations are increasingly being held accountable for their role in perpetuating racism. Movements such as OscarsSoWhite and MeToo have brought attention to the lack of diversity and the prevalence of discrimination in the entertainment industry. These movements have led to greater scrutiny and efforts to implement more inclusive practices in media production and hiring.

Technology and Social Media

Technology and social media have become powerful tools in the fight against racism, providing platforms for marginalized voices and enabling rapid mobilization for social justice causes.

Social Media Activism: Social media platforms like Twitter, Instagram, and Facebook have facilitated the spread of information and the organization of social movements. Hashtags such as BlackLivesMatter, SayHerName, and StopAsianHate have raised awareness about racial injustices and galvanized global support for anti-racist initiatives. Social media allows for the rapid dissemination of information and the coordination of protests and advocacy efforts.

Digital Storytelling: Technology has enabled new forms of digital storytelling that highlight the experiences of marginalized communities. Blogs, podcasts, and

YouTube channels created by people of color provide alternative narratives and challenge mainstream media's portrayal of race and ethnicity. These platforms allow for more diverse voices to be heard and foster a greater understanding of the complexities of racial identity.

Algorithmic Accountability: While technology can be a force for good, it can also perpetuate hidden forms of racism through biased algorithms and data practices. Efforts to address algorithmic bias and promote ethical AI development are crucial for ensuring that technology serves as a tool for inclusion rather than discrimination. This includes conducting bias audits, diversifying tech teams, and implementing transparency and accountability measures in tech companies.

International Efforts

The fight against racism is a global one, and international efforts play a critical role in advancing racial equality and promoting human rights.

Global Movements: International movements for racial justice, such as the anti-apartheid movement in South Africa and the fight for indigenous rights in various countries, have had a significant impact on advancing racial equality. These movements demonstrate the power of global solidarity and the importance of international collaboration in addressing systemic racism.

United Nations Initiatives: The United Nations has been instrumental in promoting racial equality through initiatives such as the International Decade for People of African Descent (2015-2024). This initiative aims to promote recognition, justice, and development for people of African descent worldwide. The UN's efforts to address racism and promote human rights provide a framework for member states to implement policies that advance racial equality.

Regional Organizations: Regional organizations, such as the African Union and the European Union, also play a crucial role in addressing racism. These organizations work to promote human rights, implement anti-discrimination policies, and support member states in their efforts to achieve racial equality. By fostering regional collaboration and sharing best practices, these organizations can help to create a more inclusive and equitable world.

The Importance of Sustained Activism

Sustained activism is essential for driving long-term change and ensuring that progress towards racial equality continues.

Grassroots Movements: Grassroots movements are the backbone of sustained activism. These movements are often led by marginalized communities themselves and focus on addressing local issues of racism and discrimination. Grassroots activists work tirelessly to raise awareness, mobilize communities, and advocate for policy changes that promote equity and justice.

Policy Advocacy: Advocacy for policy changes at the local, national, and international levels is crucial for addressing systemic racism. Activists work to influence legislation, hold policymakers accountable, and push for reforms that dismantle discriminatory practices and structures. Successful policy advocacy requires a combination of research, public education, and strategic lobbying.

Coalition Building: Building coalitions across different social justice movements can amplify the impact of activism. By working together, organizations and activists can pool resources, share strategies, and create a united front against racism and discrimination. Coalition building is essential for creating a broad-based movement that can address the interconnected nature of social injustices.

Areas for Improvement

Despite the progress made, there are still areas where significant improvements are needed to achieve true racial equality.

Economic Equity: Addressing economic disparities requires targeted policies and programs that promote wealth-building opportunities for marginalized communities. This includes access to affordable housing, quality education, and fair employment practices. Economic equity is essential for creating a foundation of stability and opportunity for all individuals.

Healthcare Access: Ensuring equitable access to healthcare involves addressing both systemic barriers and social determinants of health. This includes expanding access to healthcare services, promoting cultural competence among healthcare providers, and addressing the socioeconomic factors that contribute to health disparities.

Education Reform: Education systems must continue to evolve to become more inclusive and equitable. This includes addressing funding disparities, promoting diverse curricula, and implementing policies that support the academic success of all students. Education reform is critical for providing equal opportunities and empowering future generations.

Criminal Justice Reform: Comprehensive criminal justice reform is essential for addressing racial disparities in policing, sentencing, and incarceration. This includes ending discriminatory practices, promoting alternatives to incarceration, and ensuring accountability for law enforcement. Criminal justice reform is necessary for creating a system that is fair and just for all individuals.

As we continue to evaluate whether things are getting better in the fight against racism, it is important to consider the perspectives of marginalized communities and analyze both the progress and setbacks that have occurred. This section delves into specific case studies and highlights the importance of intersectionality in understanding the complexities of racial equality.

Case Study: Police Reform in the United States

The killing of George Floyd in 2020 sparked a global movement for police reform and racial justice. This case study examines the progress made and the ongoing challenges in reforming policing practices in the United States.

Progress and Reforms: Following widespread protests, several cities and states have implemented reforms aimed at increasing police accountability and reducing the use of excessive force. These reforms include the banning of chokeholds, the implementation of body camera mandates, and the establishment of civilian oversight boards. Additionally, the George Floyd Justice in Policing Act, which aims to address police misconduct and racial bias, was introduced at the federal level, though it has yet to be passed into law.

Challenges: Despite these efforts, significant challenges remain. Police unions often resist reforms, and there is a lack of uniform standards across different jurisdictions. Moreover, deep-seated issues such as systemic racism within law enforcement and the broader criminal justice system require more comprehensive and sustained efforts to address. Community trust in the police remains low in many minority neighborhoods, highlighting the need for continued advocacy and reform.

Case Study: Education Equity in the United Kingdom

Education equity is a critical issue in the fight against racism. This case study explores the progress made and the ongoing challenges in promoting educational equity for minority students in the United Kingdom.

Progress and Initiatives: The UK has made strides in addressing educational disparities through policies aimed at increasing access to quality education for minority students. Initiatives such as the Pupil Premium, which provides additional funding to schools for disadvantaged students, and the focus on closing the attainment gap have shown positive impacts. Additionally, efforts to decolonize the curriculum and include more diverse perspectives in educational materials are gaining momentum.

Challenges: Despite these efforts, significant challenges remain. Minority students, particularly Black and Asian students, continue to face disparities in academic achievement and opportunities. Issues such as implicit bias among teachers, unequal access to resources, and exclusionary disciplinary practices contribute to these disparities. Further efforts are needed to ensure that all students have equitable access to quality education and the support they need to succeed.

The Role of Intersectionality

Intersectionality is a framework for understanding how multiple social identities, such as race, gender, class, and sexuality, intersect to create unique experiences of discrimination and privilege. This section explores the importance of intersectionality in the fight against racism.

Understanding Complex Identities: Intersectionality helps us recognize that individuals do not experience racism in isolation but rather in conjunction with other forms of discrimination. For example, a Black woman may face both racial and gender discrimination, which intersect to create unique challenges. Acknowledging these complexities is essential for developing comprehensive strategies to address systemic inequalities.

Targeted Strategies: Addressing intersectional discrimination requires targeted strategies that consider the specific needs and experiences of different groups. This includes policies and programs that address the unique challenges faced by individuals at the intersection of multiple marginalized identities. By adopting an intersectional approach, we can create more inclusive and effective solutions.

Advocacy and Solidarity: Building solidarity across different social justice movements is crucial for addressing intersectional discrimination. This involves recognizing the interconnected nature of various forms of oppression and working together to advocate for comprehensive change. Collaborative efforts can amplify the impact of advocacy and create a united front against systemic inequalities.

Global Perspectives on Racial Equality

Racism is a global issue, and different countries have made varying degrees of progress in addressing it. This section explores the perspectives and experiences of different countries in the fight against racism.

South Africa: South Africa's history of apartheid and the subsequent efforts to dismantle systemic racism provide valuable lessons. The Truth and Reconciliation Commission (TRC), established in the 1990s, aimed to address the atrocities committed during apartheid and promote national healing. While the TRC made significant strides in acknowledging past injustices, ongoing issues such as economic inequality and social divisions highlight the need for continued efforts to achieve true racial equality.

Brazil: Brazil's history of slavery and racial mixing has created a complex racial landscape. Despite the country's reputation for racial harmony, significant disparities persist, particularly for Afro-Brazilians. Initiatives such as affirmative action policies in education and employment aim to address these disparities, but ongoing challenges include police violence, discrimination, and economic inequality.

Canada: Canada has made efforts to address the legacy of colonization and the treatment of Indigenous peoples through initiatives such as the Truth and Reconciliation Commission of Canada. While these efforts have raised awareness and promoted healing, Indigenous communities continue to face significant challenges, including health disparities, lack of access to education, and land rights issues. Continued advocacy and policy reforms are needed to support Indigenous rights and promote equity.

The Role of Media and Culture

Media and culture play a crucial role in shaping societal attitudes and perceptions about race. This section explores the impact of media representation and cultural expression in promoting racial equality.

Positive Representation: Positive and diverse representation in media can challenge stereotypes and promote a more inclusive understanding of different racial and ethnic groups. Films, television shows, and literature that highlight the experiences and contributions of marginalized communities can foster empathy and understanding. Efforts to increase diversity in media production and content are essential for creating a more inclusive cultural landscape.

Cultural Expression: Cultural expression through art, music, dance, and literature has always been a powerful tool for resistance and empowerment. Celebrating the cultural contributions of marginalized communities not only honours their heritage but also challenges dominant narratives and promotes a more inclusive society. Supporting cultural initiatives and providing platforms for diverse voices are crucial for fostering cultural expression and inclusion.

Media Literacy: Promoting media literacy is essential for helping individuals critically analyze media content and recognize hidden biases. Education programs that teach media literacy skills can empower individuals to challenge discriminatory portrayals and advocate for more accurate and inclusive representation.

As we continue to explore the progress made in the fight against racism, it is essential to delve into the importance of education, the role of youth, and the impact of policy changes. By examining these areas, we can gain a comprehensive understanding of the multifaceted efforts required to achieve racial equality and identify the strategies that are proving effective.

The Importance of Education

Education is a powerful tool in combating racism and promoting equity. It shapes individuals' understanding of the world and influences societal attitudes. Efforts to integrate anti-racist education and inclusive curricula are crucial in fostering a more equitable society.

Inclusive Curricula: Implementing inclusive curricula that reflect diverse perspectives and histories is essential. This involves teaching students about the contributions and experiences of marginalized communities, as well as the history of racism and its impact. By providing a more comprehensive and accurate portrayal of history, educators can help students develop a deeper understanding of racial issues and foster empathy and respect for all cultures.

Anti-Racist Education: Anti-racist education goes beyond inclusive curricula to actively challenge and dismantle racism. This includes teaching students to recognize and confront their own biases, understanding the systemic nature of racism, and equipping them with the tools to advocate for equity and justice. Schools and universities are increasingly adopting anti-racist education programs to create a more inclusive and supportive learning environment.

Teacher Training: Providing teachers with the training and resources to effectively deliver inclusive and anti-racist education is crucial. This includes professional development programs that focus on cultural competence, implicit bias, and strategies for creating inclusive classrooms. Well-trained educators are better equipped to support diverse students and promote an equitable educational experience.

The Role of Youth in Advancing Racial Equality

Youth play a vital role in the fight against racism. Their energy, creativity, and commitment to social justice are driving forces for change. Engaging and empowering young people is essential for sustaining the momentum of the movement for racial equality.

Youth-Led Movements: Youth-led movements, such as the student protests against gun violence and climate change, have demonstrated the power of young people in advocating for social change. In the context of racial equality, movements like the Black Lives Matter Youth Vanguard have mobilized young people to take action against racism and police violence. These movements highlight the importance of youth voices in shaping the future of racial justice.

Educational Programs: Educational programs that focus on leadership development, civic engagement, and social justice are essential for empowering young people. These programs provide young people with the skills and knowledge to become effective advocates for racial equality. By investing in youth education and leadership, communities can ensure that the fight for racial justice continues into the future.

Youth Mentorship: Mentorship programs that connect young people with experienced advocates and leaders can provide valuable guidance and support. Mentorship helps young people navigate the challenges of activism and develop the skills needed to lead successful campaigns. By fostering intergenerational collaboration, mentorship programs can strengthen the movement for racial equality.

The Impact of Policy Changes

Policy changes at the local, national, and international levels are crucial for addressing systemic racism and promoting equity. These changes involve reforming existing policies and implementing new ones that support marginalized communities.

Local Policies: Local governments play a key role in advancing racial equality through policies that address specific community needs. This can include initiatives such as affordable housing programs, community policing reforms, and funding for local education and healthcare services. Local policy changes can have a direct and immediate impact on the lives of marginalized individuals.

National Legislation: National legislation is essential for creating broad and lasting change. Laws that protect against discrimination, promote economic equity, and ensure access to education and healthcare are critical for addressing systemic racism. Advocates must continue to push for comprehensive legislation that addresses the root causes of racial inequality.

International Efforts: International organizations and agreements can also play a significant role in advancing racial equality. Initiatives such as the United Nations' Sustainable Development Goals (SDGs) include targets aimed at reducing inequality and promoting social justice globally. By collaborating on an international level, countries can share best practices and support each other in the fight against racism.

Case Study: Policy Changes in New Zealand

New Zealand provides an example of how policy changes can promote racial equality and support indigenous rights. The country has made significant strides in recognizing and addressing the historical and ongoing injustices faced by the Māori people.

Treaty of Waitangi Settlements: The Treaty of Waitangi, signed in 1840 between the British Crown and Māori chiefs, has been the foundation for addressing Māori grievances. In recent decades, the New Zealand government has worked to settle historical claims through the Waitangi Tribunal, providing financial compensation and land returns to Māori communities. These settlements aim to redress past wrongs and promote economic development and cultural revitalization for Māori.

Educational Reforms: New Zealand has also implemented educational reforms to support Maori students and promote Māori culture. This includes the establishment of Kura Kaupapa Māori (Māori-language immersion schools) and the incorporation of Māori perspectives and histories into the national curriculum. These efforts help to preserve Māori language and culture and provide Māori students with a more inclusive and supportive educational experience.

Health Initiatives: The New Zealand government has introduced health initiatives aimed at addressing disparities faced by Māori and Pasifika communities. These initiatives focus on providing culturally competent care, improving access to healthcare services, and addressing social determinants of health. By prioritizing the health needs of marginalized communities, New

Zealand is working to reduce health disparities and promote equity.

The Importance of Continued Advocacy

Continued advocacy is essential for maintaining progress and ensuring that policy changes are effectively implemented. Advocacy efforts must be sustained to hold governments and institutions accountable and to push for further reforms.

Grassroots Advocacy: Grassroots advocacy remains a critical component of the movement for racial equality. Community-based organizations and activists work tirelessly to raise awareness, mobilize support, and advocate for policy changes. Grassroots advocacy ensures that the voices of marginalized communities are heard and that their needs are addressed.

Public Awareness Campaigns: Public awareness campaigns play a crucial role in educating the broader public about racial issues and the importance of equity and inclusion. These campaigns can take various forms, including social media initiatives, public service announcements, and community events. By raising awareness and fostering dialogue, public awareness campaigns help to build a more informed and engaged society.

Coalition Building: Building coalitions across different social justice movements can amplify the impact of advocacy efforts. By working together, organizations and activists can create a united front against systemic racism and advocate for comprehensive reforms. Coalition building promotes solidarity and strengthens the movement for racial equality.

While significant progress has been made in the fight against racism, substantial disparities and challenges remain. Evaluating progress requires a comprehensive approach that considers both quantitative and qualitative measures, as well as an intersectional and global perspective. Ongoing efforts by governments, institutions, communities, and individuals are essential for advancing racial equality and creating a more just and inclusive world.

In the next chapter, we will explore what needs to change to achieve true racial equality. By identifying the areas where reforms are needed and discussing strategies for promoting equity, we can develop a roadmap for creating a more inclusive society.

Continuing our exploration of whether things are getting better in the fight against racism, it is essential to delve deeper into specific areas where progress has been made and identify ongoing challenges. This section will focus on the role of media, technology, and international efforts in advancing racial equality, as well as the importance of sustained activism and policy changes.

Chapter 13: What Needs to Change

To achieve true racial equality, significant changes are needed at both systemic and individual levels. This chapter outlines the key areas where reforms are necessary and discusses strategies for promoting equity. By addressing these critical issues, we can develop a roadmap for creating a more inclusive society.

Education Reform

Education is a powerful tool for social change, and reforming the education system is essential for promoting racial equality.

Equitable Funding: Ensuring that schools serving minority and low-income communities receive equitable funding is crucial. This involves addressing disparities in school funding formulas and providing additional resources to schools that need them the most. Equitable funding can help bridge the gap in educational outcomes and provide all students with the opportunities they deserve.

Inclusive Curricula: Implementing inclusive curricula that reflect the diverse histories and contributions of all racial and ethnic groups is essential. This includes teaching about the history of racism, the civil rights movement, and the experiences of marginalized communities. By providing a more comprehensive education, schools can help students develop a deeper understanding of social justice and empathy for others.

Teacher Training: Providing teachers with ongoing professional development on cultural competence, implicit bias, and anti-racist teaching practices is crucial. Well-trained educators are better equipped to create inclusive classrooms, support diverse students, and challenge discriminatory behaviours.

Addressing Disciplinary Disparities: Schools must address disparities in disciplinary practices that disproportionately affect students of color. Implementing restorative justice practices can help create a more supportive and equitable school environment. Restorative justice focuses on repairing harm and building relationships rather than punitive measures, which can reduce suspensions and expulsions.

Criminal Justice Reform

Comprehensive criminal justice reform is necessary to address systemic racism and promote fairness and equity within the legal system.

Policing Practices: Reforming policing practices to address racial biases and reduce the use of excessive force is essential. This includes implementing bias training for officers, promoting community policing initiatives, and increasing transparency and accountability in law enforcement. Additionally, policies such as banning chokeholds and limiting the use of no-knock warrants can help prevent unnecessary violence.

Sentencing Reform: Addressing racial disparities in sentencing is critical for achieving justice. This involves eliminating mandatory minimum sentences, revising three-strikes laws, and promoting alternatives to incarceration for non-violent offenses. Sentencing reform can help reduce mass incarceration and provide individuals with more opportunities for rehabilitation and reintegration into society.

Restorative Justice Programs: Implementing restorative justice programs within the criminal justice system can provide a more equitable approach to addressing harm. These programs focus on repairing the damage caused by criminal behaviour and fostering understanding between victims and offenders. Restorative justice can help reduce recidivism and promote healing within communities.

Decriminalization and Legalization: Decriminalizing certain offenses, such as drug possession, and legalizing activities that disproportionately affect minority communities can help reduce the burden on the criminal justice system and address racial disparities. By shifting the focus from punishment to public health and support, these policies can promote more equitable outcomes.

Economic Equity

Addressing economic disparities is essential for promoting racial equality and providing all individuals with the opportunities they need to thrive.

Wealth Redistribution: Implementing policies that promote wealth redistribution, such as progressive taxation and inheritance taxes, can help address the racial wealth gap. These policies can provide funding for social programs and investments in marginalized communities, promoting economic equity.

Affordable Housing: Ensuring access to affordable housing is crucial for addressing economic disparities. This involves increasing funding for affordable housing programs, implementing rent control policies, and promoting inclusive zoning practices. Affordable housing initiatives can help reduce homelessness and provide stable living conditions for marginalized individuals and families.

Job Training and Employment Programs: Providing job training and employment programs that focus on high-demand industries can help address unemployment and underemployment in marginalized communities. These programs should include support for skills development, job placement services, and partnerships with employers to create pathways to stable, well-paying jobs.

Small Business Support: Supporting minority-owned small businesses through grants, loans, and technical assistance can help promote economic growth and entrepreneurship within marginalized communities. Small businesses are essential for creating jobs and building wealth, and targeted support can help address historical disparities in access to capital and resources.

Healthcare Equity

Ensuring equitable access to healthcare is essential for addressing health disparities and promoting overall well-being.

Universal Healthcare: Implementing a universal healthcare system can help ensure that all individuals have access to necessary medical services, regardless of their economic status. Universal healthcare can reduce disparities in health outcomes and provide a foundation for equitable health services.

Cultural Competence Training: Providing cultural competence training for healthcare providers is crucial for addressing implicit biases and ensuring that all patients receive respectful and effective care. This training can help healthcare professionals understand the unique needs of diverse populations and improve patient-provider relationships.

Community Health Initiatives: Supporting community health initiatives that focus on prevention, education, and access to care can help address health disparities. These initiatives should involve community members in the planning and implementation process to ensure that they meet the specific needs of the population.

Addressing Social Determinants of Health: Addressing the social determinants of health, such as housing, education, and employment, is essential for promoting health equity. Policies that improve living conditions and provide support for marginalized communities can have a significant impact on health outcomes.

Addressing Systemic Racism

Systemic racism permeates various aspects of society, and addressing it requires comprehensive and sustained efforts.

Institutional Accountability: Holding institutions accountable for discriminatory practices and outcomes is essential for addressing systemic racism. This involves implementing regular audits, collecting and analyzing data on disparities, and enforcing anti-discrimination policies. Institutions must be transparent about their efforts and outcomes to build trust and promote accountability.

Policy Reforms: Implementing policy reforms that promote equity and address systemic barriers is crucial. This includes revising laws and regulations that disproportionately affect marginalized communities, such as those related to housing, employment, and criminal justice. Policymakers must engage with affected communities to ensure that reforms are effective and inclusive.

Community Engagement: Engaging with communities to understand their needs and perspectives is essential for developing effective solutions. This involves creating platforms for dialogue, supporting grassroots initiatives, and involving community members in decision-making processes. Community engagement fosters collaboration and ensures that policies and programs are responsive to the needs of marginalized populations.

Education and Awareness: Raising awareness about systemic racism and its impact is crucial for fostering understanding and promoting change. Education programs, public awareness campaigns, and media representation play key roles in challenging stereotypes and promoting a more inclusive society.

Conclusion

Achieving true racial equality requires comprehensive and sustained efforts across various sectors of society. Education reform, criminal justice reform, economic equity, healthcare equity, and addressing systemic racism are all critical components of this process. By implementing targeted strategies and promoting collaboration, we can develop a roadmap for creating a more inclusive and equitable society.
In the next chapter, we will explore what we can do together to promote racial equality and support marginalized communities. By identifying actionable steps and fostering collective action, we can work towards a more just and inclusive world.

To further understand what needs to change to achieve true racial equality, it is essential to explore specific strategies and actions that can be taken at individual, community, and institutional levels. This section focuses on actionable steps that can be implemented to promote equity and support marginalized communities.

Individual Actions

Individual actions, while seemingly small, collectively contribute to significant social change. Everyone has a role to play in combating racism and promoting inclusivity.

Self-Education: Individuals should commit to ongoing self-education about racism and its impact. This includes reading books, watching documentaries, and engaging with resources that provide diverse perspectives. Understanding the history and current manifestations of racism is crucial for effective allyship.

Challenging Biases: People must recognize and challenge their own biases. This involves reflecting on personal prejudices, engaging in conversations about race, and being open to feedback. Tools such as implicit bias tests can help individuals identify and address unconscious biases.

Speaking Out: Speaking out against racist behaviours and comments is essential. This can involve challenging friends, family members, or colleagues when they express racist views, as well as publicly supporting anti-racist initiatives. Silence can perpetuate racism, so using one's voice to advocate for justice is crucial.

Supporting Marginalized Communities: Individuals can support marginalized communities through actions such as volunteering, donating to relevant causes, and supporting minority-owned businesses. Engaging with and supporting community organizations that work towards racial justice can have a meaningful impact.

Community-Level Actions

Communities play a vital role in fostering inclusivity and addressing local issues of racism. Community-level actions can create supportive environments and promote equity.

Creating Safe Spaces: Communities should create safe spaces for dialogue and support. This includes organizing forums, support groups, and town hall meetings where individuals can share their experiences and discuss strategies for promoting racial justice. Safe spaces allow for open and honest conversations about race and help build solidarity.

Promoting Cultural Competence: Community organizations should provide cultural competence training for members and leaders. This training can help individuals understand and respect cultural differences, reducing misunderstandings and promoting inclusivity.

Supporting Grassroots Movements: Grassroots movements often address specific local issues and have a deep understanding of community needs. Supporting these movements through funding, resources, and volunteer efforts can help advance racial justice at the community level.

Implementing Community Programs: Developing and implementing programs that address the specific needs of marginalized communities is crucial. This can include educational programs, mentorship initiatives, health clinics, and economic empowerment projects. Tailored programs can effectively address disparities and support community development.

Institutional Actions

Institutions, from businesses to government agencies, have a significant impact on societal norms and practices. Institutional actions are essential for systemic change.

Implementing Anti-Racist Policies: Institutions should implement comprehensive anti-racist policies that address discrimination and promote equity. This includes hiring practices, workplace culture, and service delivery. Policies should be regularly reviewed and updated to ensure they remain effective.

Diversity and Inclusion Training: Providing regular diversity and inclusion training for employees and leaders is crucial. This training should cover topics such as implicit bias, cultural competence, and anti-racist practices. Effective training can help create a more inclusive and supportive institutional environment.

Accountability Measures: Institutions must establish accountability measures to ensure that anti-racist policies and practices are enforced. This includes creating oversight bodies, conducting regular audits, and establishing channels for reporting and addressing discrimination.

Supporting Minority Leadership: Promoting diversity in leadership positions is essential for fostering inclusive institutions. This involves actively recruiting and supporting minority candidates for leadership roles and creating pathways for career advancement.

 Policy and Legislative Actions
Policy and legislative actions at the local, national, and international levels are critical for addressing systemic racism and promoting equity.

Anti-Discrimination Laws: Enacting and enforcing robust anti-discrimination laws is essential for protecting the rights of marginalized individuals. These laws should cover areas such as employment, housing, education, and public services. Ensuring that these laws are effectively enforced is crucial for their impact.

Equitable Funding: Governments should allocate equitable funding to programs and services that support marginalized communities. This includes education, healthcare, housing, and economic development initiatives. Equitable funding can help address disparities and promote social mobility.

Criminal Justice Reform: Comprehensive criminal justice reform is necessary to address systemic biases and ensure fairness. This includes revising sentencing laws, promoting alternatives to incarceration, and implementing community-based policing practices. Reform efforts should focus on reducing disparities and promoting rehabilitation.

International Collaboration: International collaboration on racial justice issues can amplify efforts and promote shared learning. Countries should work together to implement best practices, support international human rights initiatives, and hold each other accountable for progress.

The Role of Media and Technology

Media and technology have the power to shape public perceptions and influence societal attitudes. Leveraging these tools effectively can promote racial equality and challenge discriminatory practices.

Positive Representation: Media organizations should strive for positive and accurate representation of diverse racial and ethnic groups. This includes diversifying content creators, promoting stories that reflect a wide range of experiences, and challenging stereotypes. Positive representation can help normalize diversity and foster empathy.

Combating Misinformation: Addressing misinformation and harmful narratives about race is crucial. Media outlets and technology platforms should implement measures to identify and counteract false information and hate speech. Promoting accurate and balanced reporting can contribute to a more informed and inclusive society.

Digital Activism: Social media and digital platforms provide powerful tools for activism and advocacy. Activists can use these platforms to raise awareness, mobilize support, and advocate for policy changes. Supporting digital activism through access to resources and training can amplify its impact.

Algorithmic Fairness: Technology companies must address biases in algorithms and ensure that their products do not perpetuate discrimination. This involves conducting regular audits, diversifying development teams, and implementing ethical guidelines for AI and machine learning.

As we continue to explore what needs to change to achieve true racial equality, it is important to delve deeper into the role of leadership, the importance of allyship, and the power of collective action. By understanding these elements, we can create a comprehensive approach to dismantling racism and promoting equity.

The Role of Leadership

Effective leadership is crucial for driving change and fostering an inclusive society. Leaders in various sectors must commit to promoting racial equality and creating environments where everyone can thrive.

Inclusive Leadership: Inclusive leaders prioritize diversity and inclusion in their decision-making processes. They actively seek out and value diverse perspectives, create policies that promote equity, and hold themselves and others accountable for fostering an inclusive environment. Inclusive leadership involves leading by example and demonstrating a commitment to social justice.

Representation in Leadership: Increasing representation of marginalized groups in leadership positions is essential for promoting equity. This involves actively recruiting and supporting individuals from diverse backgrounds for leadership roles. Representation matters because it ensures that decision-makers reflect the communities they serve and can address the unique challenges faced by marginalized groups.

Mentorship and Sponsorship: Leaders should provide mentorship and sponsorship to individuals from underrepresented groups. Mentorship programs can offer guidance, support, and professional development opportunities, while sponsorship involves advocating for the advancement of protégés within the organization. These initiatives help build a pipeline of diverse leaders and promote career advancement.

Transparency and Accountability: Leaders must be transparent about their efforts to promote racial equality and hold themselves accountable for progress. This involves setting measurable goals, regularly reporting on outcomes, and being open to feedback. Accountability mechanisms, such as diversity councils or external audits, can help ensure that commitments to equity are met.

The Importance of Allyship

Allyship involves individuals from privileged groups actively supporting and advocating for marginalized communities. Effective allyship requires ongoing self-reflection, education, and action.

Listening and Learning: Allies must prioritize listening to the experiences and perspectives of marginalized individuals. This involves seeking out diverse voices, being open to feedback, and continuously educating themselves about issues of racism and discrimination. Listening and learning are foundational steps in becoming an effective ally.

Using Privilege for Good: Allies can leverage their privilege to advocate for change and support marginalized communities. This includes amplifying marginalized voices, challenging discriminatory behaviours, and advocating for equitable policies. Allies should use their platforms and influence to raise awareness and drive progress.

Taking Action: Allyship requires taking concrete actions to combat racism and promote inclusion. This can involve participating in protests, supporting anti-racist organizations, and advocating for policy changes. Allies should be proactive in their efforts and committed to sustained action.

Building Relationships: Building genuine relationships with individuals from marginalized communities is essential for effective allyship. These relationships should be based on mutual respect, trust, and a commitment to supporting one another. Allies should prioritize building meaningful connections and learning from those directly affected by racism.

The Power of Collective Action

Collective action involves individuals and groups working together to achieve common goals. In the fight against racism, collective action can amplify efforts and create significant social change.

Building Coalitions: Building coalitions across different social justice movements can strengthen advocacy efforts and create a united front against systemic racism. Coalitions bring together diverse perspectives, resources, and strategies, enhancing the overall impact of the movement. Collaborative efforts can address the interconnected nature of social injustices and promote comprehensive solutions.

Community Organizing: Community organizing involves mobilizing individuals and groups to advocate for change at the local level. This includes organizing protests, campaigns, and events that raise awareness and push for policy changes. Community organizers play a crucial role in building grassroots movements and fostering local engagement.

Supporting Advocacy Groups: Supporting advocacy groups that work towards racial justice is essential for sustaining the movement. This includes providing financial support, volunteering, and amplifying their messages. Advocacy groups often have the expertise and resources needed to drive policy changes and support marginalized communities.

Engaging in Dialogue: Open and honest dialogue about race and racism is crucial for building understanding and solidarity. Creating spaces for dialogue, such as community forums, workshops, and discussion groups, can foster meaningful conversations and promote empathy. Dialogue can help bridge divides and create a shared commitment to racial justice.

Strategies for Sustained Change

Achieving sustained change requires a long-term commitment and a multifaceted approach. By implementing targeted strategies and fostering collaboration, we can create a more inclusive and equitable society.

Policy Advocacy: Advocating for policy changes that promote racial equality is essential for creating systemic change. This involves pushing for anti-discrimination laws, equitable funding, and comprehensive criminal justice reform. Policy advocacy requires a combination of research, public education, and strategic lobbying.

Public Education Campaigns: Public education campaigns can raise awareness about racial issues and promote understanding and empathy. These campaigns can take various forms, including social media initiatives, public service announcements, and community events. Effective public education campaigns can challenge stereotypes and foster a more informed and inclusive society.

Supporting Research and Data Collection: Supporting research and data collection on racial disparities is crucial for developing evidence-based solutions. Research can provide valuable insights into the root causes of inequality and inform policy decisions. Data collection efforts should prioritize transparency and inclusivity, ensuring that the voices of marginalized communities are represented.

Promoting Cultural Competence: Promoting cultural competence in all sectors of society can help create more inclusive environments. This involves providing training and resources that help individuals understand and respect cultural differences. Cultural competence initiatives should be ongoing and integrated into organizational practices.

In the final segment of this chapter, we will explore how various sectors of society can contribute to promoting racial equality and dismantling systemic racism. By focusing on education, healthcare, corporate responsibility, and media, we can identify actionable steps that institutions and individuals can take to create a more inclusive world.

Education

Education systems have a profound impact on shaping societal values and fostering understanding. Implementing comprehensive strategies to address racism within education is crucial for long-term change.

Inclusive Curriculum Development: Schools and universities should develop curricula that include the histories and contributions of marginalized communities. This includes incorporating the experiences of people of color into subjects such as history, literature, and social studies. An inclusive curriculum helps students understand the diverse fabric of society and the historical context of racism.

Bias Training for Educators: Providing bias training for educators can help them recognize and mitigate their own prejudices. This training should cover topics such as implicit bias, cultural competence, and strategies for creating inclusive classrooms. Educators equipped with this knowledge can better support all students and foster an equitable learning environment.

Equity in Resources: Ensuring that schools in marginalized communities receive equitable funding and resources is essential. This includes access to advanced coursework, extracurricular activities, and technology. Equitable resource allocation can help bridge the achievement gap and provide all students with the opportunities they need to succeed.

Support Services for Students: Implementing support services, such as counselling and mentorship programs, can help students from marginalized communities navigate the challenges they face. These services should be culturally responsive and accessible to all students. Support services can promote mental health, academic success, and overall well-being.

Healthcare

Addressing racial disparities in healthcare requires a multi-faceted approach that includes policy changes, education, and community engagement.

Universal Healthcare Access: Ensuring universal access to healthcare is fundamental for addressing disparities. Policymakers should work towards implementing healthcare systems that provide comprehensive coverage for all individuals, regardless of their economic status. Universal healthcare can reduce health disparities and promote equity.

Cultural Competence in Healthcare: Healthcare providers should receive training on cultural competence to better understand and address the needs of diverse populations. This training should cover communication skills, cultural awareness, and the social determinants of health. Culturally competent care can improve patient outcomes and reduce disparities.

Community Health Programs: Developing community health programs that focus on prevention, education, and access to care is essential. These programs should involve community members in their design and implementation to ensure they meet the specific needs of the population. Community health programs can promote wellness and reduce health disparities.

Addressing Social Determinants of Health: Policies that address the social determinants of health, such as housing, education, and employment, are crucial for promoting health equity. Efforts to improve living conditions and provide support for marginalized communities can have a significant impact on health outcomes.

Corporate Responsibility

Corporations have a significant influence on societal norms and practices. By committing to diversity, equity, and inclusion, businesses can play a pivotal role in promoting racial equality.

Diverse Hiring Practices: Corporations should implement hiring practices that promote diversity and inclusion. This includes using blind recruitment processes, setting diversity goals, and actively recruiting candidates from underrepresented groups. Diverse hiring practices can create more inclusive workplaces and promote equity.

Inclusive Workplace Culture: Creating an inclusive workplace culture involves implementing policies and practices that support all employees. This includes providing diversity and inclusion training, establishing employee resource groups, and promoting work-life balance. An inclusive workplace culture can enhance employee satisfaction and productivity.

Corporate Accountability: Corporations should be held accountable for their diversity and inclusion efforts. This involves setting measurable goals, regularly reporting on progress, and being transparent about challenges and successes. Accountability mechanisms, such as diversity audits and external reviews, can help ensure that commitments to equity are met.

Community Engagement: Businesses should engage with the communities they serve and support local initiatives that promote racial justice. This can include partnerships with community organizations, sponsorship of events, and volunteer programs. Community engagement helps build trust and supports broader social change.

Media

Media has the power to shape public perceptions and influence societal attitudes. Promoting diversity and inclusion in media is essential for challenging stereotypes and fostering understanding.

Representation in Media: Media organizations should strive for diverse representation in their content. This includes featuring stories and characters from different racial and ethnic backgrounds and ensuring that diverse voices are heard. Representation matters because it helps normalize diversity and fosters empathy.

Combating Misinformation: Media outlets should work to combat misinformation and harmful narratives about race. This involves fact-checking, providing balanced reporting, and highlighting stories that challenge stereotypes. Accurate and responsible journalism can promote a more informed and inclusive society.

Supporting Diverse Creators: Supporting creators from marginalized communities is crucial for promoting diversity in media. This includes providing funding, resources, and platforms for diverse voices. Supporting diverse creators helps ensure that a wide range of experiences and perspectives are represented.

Media Literacy: Promoting media literacy is essential for helping individuals critically analyze media content and recognize biases. Education programs that teach media literacy skills can empower audiences to challenge discriminatory portrayals and advocate for more inclusive representation.

Conclusion

Achieving true racial equality requires comprehensive and sustained efforts across various sectors of society. By focusing on education, healthcare, corporate responsibility, and media, we can identify actionable steps that institutions and individuals can take to promote equity and support marginalized communities. Effective leadership, allyship, and collective action are critical components of this process. By implementing targeted strategies and fostering collaboration, we can create a roadmap for a more inclusive and equitable society.

In the next chapter, we will explore what we can do together to promote racial equality and support marginalized communities. By identifying actionable steps and fostering collective action, we can work towards a more just and inclusive world.

Chapter 14: What We Can Do Together

Promoting racial equality and supporting marginalized communities requires collective action and a commitment to sustained efforts. This chapter explores how individuals, communities, institutions, and policymakers can work together to create a more just and inclusive society. By identifying actionable steps and fostering collaboration, we can address systemic racism and promote equity.

Individual Actions

Every individual has the power to contribute to the fight against racism. By taking intentional actions, people can make a significant impact in their communities and beyond.

Educate Yourself and Others: Continuously educate yourself about the history and impact of racism. Read books, attend workshops, and engage with diverse perspectives. Share your knowledge with others and encourage open conversations about race and equity.

Support Anti-Racist Organizations: Donate to or volunteer with organizations that work towards racial justice. These organizations often rely on community support to fund their initiatives and advocacy efforts. Your contributions can help sustain their vital work.

Vote and Advocate for Policy Change: Participate in local, state, and national elections and advocate for policies that promote racial equality. Contact your representatives to express your support for anti-racist legislation and hold them accountable for their actions.

Challenge Racism in Your Daily Life: Speak out against racist comments and behaviours when you encounter them. Support friends, family, and colleagues in understanding and addressing their biases. Create inclusive environments in your personal and professional circles.

Community Actions

Communities play a crucial role in fostering inclusivity and addressing local issues of racism. By working together, community members can create supportive environments and drive meaningful change.

Organize Community Events: Host events such as town hall meetings, cultural festivals, and educational workshops that promote understanding and dialogue about race. These events can help build solidarity and raise awareness about local issues of racism.

Support Local Businesses: Patronize minority-owned businesses and encourage others to do the same. Supporting local businesses helps build economic equity and strengthens community ties.

Create Safe Spaces: Establish safe spaces where individuals from marginalized communities can share their experiences and receive support. These spaces can provide a sense of belonging and help individuals navigate the challenges they face.

Collaborate with Community Organizations: Partner with local organizations that work towards racial justice. Collaborate on initiatives, share resources, and support each other's efforts. Community partnerships can amplify the impact of your actions and create a united front against racism.

Institutional Actions

Institutions have a significant impact on societal norms and practices. By committing to diversity, equity, and inclusion, institutions can drive systemic change and create more equitable environments.

Implement Diversity and Inclusion Policies: Develop and enforce policies that promote diversity and inclusion within your institution. This includes equitable hiring practices, inclusive workplace culture, and support for minority employees.

Provide Training and Education: Offer regular training on topics such as implicit bias, cultural competence, and anti-racist practices. Ensure that all employees, from leadership to entry-level staff, receive this training.

Establish Accountability Measures: Create mechanisms to hold the institution accountable for its diversity and inclusion efforts. This includes setting measurable goals, conducting regular audits, and being transparent about progress and challenges.

Engage with the Community: Build relationships with the communities you serve and support local initiatives that promote racial justice. Engaging with the community can help institutions understand and address the specific needs and challenges faced by marginalized groups.

Policy and Legislative Actions

Policy and legislative changes are essential for addressing systemic racism and promoting equity at a broader level. Policymakers must commit to creating and enforcing laws that protect the rights of marginalized communities.

Enact Anti-Discrimination Laws: Pass and enforce robust anti-discrimination laws that cover employment, housing, education, and public services. Ensure that these laws are effectively implemented and that violators are held accountable.

Promote Economic Equity: Implement policies that address the racial wealth gap and promote economic equity. This includes progressive taxation, affordable housing programs, and support for minority-owned businesses.

Reform the Criminal Justice System: Enact comprehensive criminal justice reform to address racial disparities in policing, sentencing, and incarceration. Promote alternatives to incarceration, end discriminatory practices, and ensure accountability for law enforcement.

Support Universal Healthcare: Work towards implementing universal healthcare systems that provide comprehensive coverage for all individuals. Universal healthcare can reduce health disparities and ensure equitable access to medical services.

The Role of Media and Technology

Media and technology have the power to shape public perceptions and influence societal attitudes. Leveraging these tools effectively can promote racial equality and challenge discriminatory practices.

Promote Diverse Representation: Media organizations should strive for diverse representation in their content. This includes featuring stories and characters from different racial and ethnic backgrounds and ensuring that diverse voices are heard.

Combat Misinformation: Media outlets should work to combat misinformation and harmful narratives about race. This involves fact-checking, providing balanced reporting, and highlighting stories that challenge stereotypes.

Support Digital Activism: Social media and digital platforms provide powerful tools for activism and advocacy. Activists can use these platforms to raise awareness, mobilize support, and advocate for policy changes.

Address Algorithmic Bias: Technology companies must address biases in algorithms and ensure that their products do not perpetuate discrimination. This involves conducting regular audits, diversifying development teams, and implementing ethical guidelines for AI and machine learning.

Building a Culture of Solidarity

Creating a culture of solidarity involves fostering a sense of mutual support and shared responsibility for promoting racial equality. By building strong relationships and working together, we can create a more inclusive and equitable society.

Foster Empathy and Understanding: Encourage empathy and understanding by promoting open dialogue and active listening. Share stories and experiences that highlight the impact of racism and the importance of solidarity.

Celebrate Diversity: Celebrate the cultural contributions of all communities. Support cultural festivals, promote diverse representation in media and arts, and integrate diverse perspectives into educational curricula.

Support Intersectional Advocacy: Recognize the interconnected nature of social injustices and support intersectional advocacy efforts. Work together with other social justice movements to address issues such as gender inequality, economic disparity, and environmental justice.

Commit to Long-Term Action: Promoting racial equality requires sustained commitment and long-term action. Continue to educate yourself, support marginalized communities, and advocate for systemic change. Stay engaged and persistent in your efforts to create a more just and inclusive world.

As we delve deeper into how we can collectively promote racial equality, it is essential to highlight specific initiatives and strategies that have proven effective in fostering inclusivity and addressing systemic racism. By examining successful case studies and actionable steps, we can provide a roadmap for communities and institutions to follow.

Case Studies of Successful Initiatives

The Truth and Reconciliation Commission (TRC) of Canada: The TRC was established to address the legacy of residential schools and promote reconciliation between Indigenous peoples and the Canadian government. The Commission's work involved collecting testimonies from survivors, raising awareness about the abuses suffered, and making recommendations for systemic changes. The TRC's efforts have led to increased awareness and policy reforms aimed at addressing historical injustices.

The Equal Justice Initiative (EJI): Founded by Bryan Stevenson, the EJI focuses on criminal justice reform, particularly in addressing racial disparities in sentencing and incarceration. The EJI has been instrumental in securing legal representation for wrongly convicted individuals, advocating for policy changes, and educating the public about the history of racial injustice in the United States. Their work has led to significant legal victories and increased public awareness.

The Black Lives Matter (BLM) Movement: BLM has become a global movement advocating for an end to systemic racism and violence against Black people. Through protests, social media campaigns, and policy advocacy, BLM has brought attention to issues such as police brutality and racial inequality. The movement has influenced public discourse, led to policy changes, and inspired a new generation of activists.

 Strategies for Promoting Racial Equality

Community-Led Initiatives: Grassroots efforts driven by community members can effectively address local issues of racism. These initiatives often have a deep understanding of the specific needs and challenges faced by their communities. Examples include community organizing, local advocacy groups, and neighborhood support networks. Community-led initiatives can drive meaningful change by mobilizing local resources and fostering solidarity.

Policy Advocacy and Reform: Advocating for policy changes at all levels of government is crucial for addressing systemic racism. This includes pushing for legislation that promotes equity in education, healthcare, housing, and criminal justice. Policy advocacy involves engaging with policymakers, conducting research, and building coalitions to support legislative changes.

Educational Programs: Implementing educational programs that focus on anti-racism, cultural competence, and the history of racial injustice is essential. Schools, universities, and community organizations should offer curricula and training that educate individuals about the impact of racism and the importance of diversity and inclusion. Educational programs can foster a more informed and empathetic society.

Economic Empowerment: Addressing economic disparities requires targeted efforts to promote economic empowerment for marginalized communities. This includes supporting minority-owned businesses, providing job training and employment programs, and implementing policies that promote economic equity. Economic empowerment initiatives can help bridge the wealth gap and create opportunities for social mobility.

Building Inclusive Institutions

Diversity and Inclusion Councils: Establishing diversity and inclusion councils within institutions can help drive systemic change. These councils can assess current practices, recommend policies, and monitor progress towards diversity goals. By involving diverse voices in decision-making processes, institutions can create more inclusive environments.

Bias Incident Reporting Systems: Implementing systems for reporting and addressing bias incidents is crucial for creating safe and supportive environments. These systems should provide clear guidelines for reporting incidents, offer support to affected individuals, and ensure accountability for discriminatory behaviours. Transparent and effective reporting systems can help address issues of racism and promote a culture of inclusion.

Employee Resource Groups (ERGs): ERGs provide support and advocacy for employees from marginalized communities. These groups can offer mentorship, professional development opportunities, and a sense of community. ERGs can also provide valuable insights to leadership on how to create a more inclusive workplace culture.

Inclusive Leadership Training: Providing training for leaders on inclusive practices and cultural competence is essential for fostering an equitable institution. Leaders should be equipped with the skills to recognize and address their own biases, create inclusive policies, and support diverse teams. Inclusive leadership training can help build a more supportive and equitable organizational culture.

Engaging in Intersectional Advocacy

Recognizing Intersecting Identities: Intersectional advocacy involves understanding how different aspects of identity, such as race, gender, class, and sexuality, intersect to create unique experiences of discrimination and privilege. Effective advocacy must consider these intersections to address the full scope of systemic injustice.

Collaborating Across Movements: Building coalitions with other social justice movements can amplify efforts and create a broader impact. Collaboration allows for the sharing of resources, strategies, and support. By working together, advocates can address the interconnected nature of social injustices and promote comprehensive solutions.

Supporting Marginalized Voices: Ensuring that marginalized voices are at the forefront of advocacy efforts is crucial. This involves creating platforms for these voices to be heard, providing opportunities for leadership, and actively listening to their experiences and perspectives. Centering marginalized voices helps ensure that advocacy efforts are inclusive and effective.

Leveraging Technology for Racial Justice

Digital Activism: Social media and digital platforms provide powerful tools for raising awareness, mobilizing support, and advocating for change. Activists can use these platforms to share information, organize events, and amplify marginalized voices. Effective digital activism involves using technology to engage and educate broader audiences.

Online Education and Resources: Providing online education and resources on topics such as anti-racism, cultural competence, and the history of racial injustice can reach a wide audience. Online platforms can offer courses, webinars, and resource libraries that educate individuals and support advocacy efforts.

Addressing Digital Divide: Ensuring equitable access to technology is essential for promoting racial equality. This involves addressing the digital divide by providing access to devices, internet connectivity, and digital literacy training for marginalized communities. Equitable access to technology can support education, economic empowerment, and advocacy efforts.

As we conclude our exploration of collective actions to promote racial equality, it is crucial to consider the role of innovation, the importance of measuring progress, and the power of storytelling. These elements can enhance our efforts to address systemic racism and create lasting change.

Innovation in Promoting Racial Equality

Innovation can play a significant role in addressing systemic racism and promoting racial equality. By leveraging new technologies, creative solutions, and forward-thinking approaches, we can develop effective strategies for combating discrimination and fostering inclusivity.

Technological Solutions: Advances in technology can be harnessed to promote racial equality. For example, data analytics can be used to identify and address disparities in various sectors, such as healthcare, education, and criminal justice. Technology can also facilitate the creation of platforms that amplify marginalized voices, connect advocates, and organize collective actions.

Creative Approaches: Creative approaches to advocacy, such as art, music, and theatre, can raise awareness and inspire action. These mediums have the power to convey complex messages and evoke emotional responses, making them effective tools for promoting empathy and understanding. Supporting artists and creators from marginalized communities can help amplify their voices and contribute to the cultural movement for racial justice.

Innovation in Policy Development: Innovative policy development involves thinking beyond traditional frameworks and considering new ways to address systemic issues. This can include implementing pilot programs, using behavioural science to inform policy design, and adopting evidence-based practices. Policymakers should be open to experimenting with novel approaches and learning from successful initiatives in other contexts.

Measuring Progress and Accountability

Measuring progress and ensuring accountability are essential for evaluating the effectiveness of efforts to promote racial equality. By setting clear goals, tracking outcomes, and holding individuals and institutions accountable, we can ensure that our actions lead to meaningful change.

Setting Clear Goals: Establishing clear, measurable goals is crucial for guiding efforts and assessing progress. These goals should be specific, achievable, and aligned

with the broader objectives of promoting racial equality.
Examples include increasing diversity in leadership
positions, reducing racial disparities in healthcare
outcomes, and improving educational attainment for
marginalized students.

Tracking Outcomes: Regularly tracking outcomes and
collecting data on key indicators can help evaluate the
impact of initiatives. This involves using both
quantitative and qualitative measures to assess progress.
Quantitative data can provide insights into trends and
disparities, while qualitative data can capture the
experiences and perspectives of marginalized
individuals.

Public Reporting: Publicly reporting on progress and
outcomes is essential for transparency and
accountability. Institutions and organizations should
share their findings with stakeholders and the broader
community. Regular reporting can build trust,
demonstrate commitment to change, and encourage
continuous improvement.

Accountability Mechanisms: Establishing accountability
mechanisms ensures that commitments to racial equality
are upheld. This can include creating oversight bodies,
conducting external audits, and implementing
consequences for failing to meet goals. Accountability
mechanisms help maintain focus and drive sustained
efforts towards achieving equity.

The Power of Storytelling

Storytelling is a powerful tool for raising awareness, fostering empathy, and inspiring action. By sharing personal stories and experiences, we can humanize the issues of racism and create connections that drive collective efforts for change.

Personal Narratives: Personal narratives provide a firsthand account of the impact of racism on individuals' lives. These stories can highlight the challenges faced by marginalized communities and the resilience they demonstrate. Sharing personal narratives can build empathy and understanding, encouraging others to join the fight for racial justice.

Historical Accounts: Documenting and sharing historical accounts of racial injustice is crucial for understanding the roots of systemic racism and its enduring effects. This includes stories of resistance, activism, and progress. By learning from history, we can better understand the present and work towards a more just future.

Amplifying Marginalized Voices: Ensuring that marginalized voices are heard and amplified is essential for effective storytelling. This involves creating platforms for these voices, providing opportunities for leadership, and actively listening to their experiences and perspectives. Amplifying marginalized voices helps ensure that advocacy efforts are inclusive and grounded in the realities of those most affected by racism.

Creative Storytelling: Creative storytelling through mediums such as film, literature, and digital media can reach a wide audience and evoke powerful emotional responses. These stories can challenge stereotypes, highlight injustices, and promote a vision of a more inclusive society. Supporting diverse creators and promoting their work can contribute to the cultural movement for racial justice.

Building Sustainable Movements

Sustaining the momentum of movements for racial equality requires ongoing commitment, resources, and collaboration. By building sustainable movements, we can ensure that progress continues and that efforts are resilient in the face of challenges.

Long-Term Commitment: Promoting racial equality is a long-term endeavor that requires sustained commitment from individuals, communities, institutions, and policymakers. This involves setting long-term goals, developing strategic plans, and being prepared to adapt to changing circumstances.

Resource Allocation: Adequate resources are essential for sustaining movements and initiatives. This includes funding, staffing, and access to tools and technology. Ensuring that resources are equitably distributed and accessible to marginalized communities is crucial for supporting their efforts.

Collaboration and Partnerships: Building strong collaborations and partnerships can amplify efforts and create a broader impact. This involves working together across sectors, sharing knowledge and resources, and supporting each other's initiatives. Collaboration can help create a united front against systemic racism.

Continuous Learning and Adaptation: Continuous learning and adaptation are essential for sustaining movements. This involves regularly assessing progress, learning from successes and challenges, and being open to new ideas and approaches. By fostering a culture of learning and innovation, movements can remain dynamic and effective.

Promoting racial equality and supporting marginalized communities requires collective action, innovation, and sustained efforts. By leveraging technology, measuring progress, harnessing the power of storytelling, and building sustainable movements, we can create lasting change. Effective leadership, allyship, and collaboration are critical components of this process. By implementing targeted strategies and fostering a culture of solidarity, we can work towards a more just and inclusive world.

In the next chapter, we will reflect on the journey through this book and reiterate the importance of addressing racism in all its forms. By sharing personal reflections and a hopeful vision for the future, we aim to inspire readers to take action and contribute to the ongoing struggle for racial equality.

Chapter 15: Conclusion – A Call to Action

As we come to the end of this journey through the complexities of racism and the efforts required to combat it, it is essential to reflect on the insights gained and the actions that must follow. The fight against racism is an ongoing struggle that demands our collective commitment, empathy, and resilience. This concluding chapter serves as a call to action, urging readers to take meaningful steps towards promoting racial equality and justice.

Personal Reflections

Writing this book has been a deeply personal and enlightening experience. It has reaffirmed my belief in the power of education, advocacy, and collective action in addressing systemic racism. I am reminded of the countless individuals and communities who have shown incredible resilience and strength in the face of adversity. Their stories inspire me to continue working towards a world where everyone is treated with dignity and respect.

Acknowledging Privilege: Throughout this process, I have reflected on my own privileges and the ways in which they shape my experiences and perspectives. Acknowledging privilege is a crucial step in the fight against racism, as it allows us to recognize the systemic advantages we may have and use them to advocate for equity.

The Importance of Empathy: Empathy is a powerful tool in combating racism. By listening to and understanding the experiences of others, we can build stronger connections and foster a more inclusive society. Empathy drives us to take action and stand in solidarity with marginalized communities.

Commitment to Action: Writing this book has reinforced my commitment to taking action against racism in all its forms. It is not enough to be passively non-racist; we must be actively anti-racist, challenging discrimination whenever and wherever we encounter it.

The Ongoing Fight for Racial Equality

The fight for racial equality is far from over. While progress has been made, significant challenges remain. It is essential to remain vigilant and continue pushing for change at every level of society.

Systemic Change: Achieving racial equality requires systemic change. This involves addressing the root causes of racism and implementing comprehensive reforms across various sectors, including education, healthcare, criminal justice, and the economy. Systemic change is a long-term endeavor that requires sustained commitment and collective effort.

Grassroots Movements: Grassroots movements play a vital role in driving social change. These movements are often led by those most affected by racism and have a deep understanding of their communities' needs.

Supporting grassroots initiatives and amplifying their voices is crucial for creating meaningful and lasting change.

Policy Advocacy: Advocacy for policy changes is essential for addressing systemic racism. This involves engaging with policymakers, building coalitions, and pushing for legislation that promotes equity and justice. Policy advocacy can lead to significant advancements in protecting the rights of marginalized communities.

A Vision for the Future

Envisioning a future free from racism requires imagination, hope, and a shared commitment to justice. While the journey ahead may be challenging, it is one that we must undertake together.

Equity and Inclusion: In this envisioned future, equity and inclusion are foundational principles. All individuals, regardless of their race or background, have equal access to opportunities and resources. Institutions and communities prioritize diversity and create environments where everyone feels valued and respected.

Solidarity and Allyship: Solidarity and allyship are central to this future. People from all backgrounds come together to support one another and work towards common goals. Allies use their privilege to amplify marginalized voices and advocate for systemic change.

Ongoing Learning and Growth: Continuous learning and growth are essential in this future. Individuals and institutions remain open to new ideas, perspectives, and approaches. They engage in ongoing self-reflection and are committed to improving their practices to promote racial equality.

Resilience and Hope: Resilience and hope are the driving forces behind this future. Despite the challenges, we remain steadfast in our commitment to justice. We draw strength from the progress made and the knowledge that our collective efforts can lead to a more just and inclusive world.

Taking Action

As we conclude this book, I urge you to take action in your own life and community. Here are some steps you can take to contribute to the fight against racism:

Educate Yourself: Continue to educate yourself about racism and its impact. Read books, attend workshops, and engage with diverse perspectives. Share your knowledge with others and encourage open conversations about race and equity.

Support Anti-Racist Organizations: Donate to or volunteer with organizations that work towards racial justice. These organizations often rely on community support to fund their initiatives and advocacy efforts.

Advocate for Policy Change: Participate in local, state, and national elections and advocate for policies that promote racial equality. Contact your representatives to express your support for anti-racist legislation and hold them accountable for their actions.

Challenge Racism in Your Daily Life: Speak out against racist behaviours and comments when you encounter them. Support friends, family, and colleagues in understanding and addressing their biases. Create inclusive environments in your personal and professional circles.

Build Inclusive Communities: Work with others in your community to create inclusive spaces and support marginalized individuals. Organize events, support local businesses, and collaborate with community organizations to promote equity and justice.

The journey to racial equality is a collective effort that requires each of us to play our part. By educating ourselves, supporting marginalized communities, advocating for policy changes, and challenging racism in our daily lives, we can contribute to a more just and inclusive world. Let us remain committed to this fight, drawing inspiration from those who have come before us and those who continue to work tirelessly for justice.

Together, we can create a future where everyone is treated with dignity and respect, where equity and inclusion are the norm, and where the fight against racism is a shared and ongoing commitment. Let us take action, support one another, and strive for a world where racial equality is a reality for all.

In this final segment, we focus on practical steps and commitments that individuals, communities, institutions, and policymakers can make to drive the fight against racism forward. By collectively embracing these actions, we can ensure that the momentum for racial equality is sustained and that our efforts lead to meaningful change.

Commitments for Individuals

Continuous Self-Education: Make a lifelong commitment to learning about racism and its effects. Regularly read books, watch documentaries, attend seminars, and engage in conversations about race and social justice. Challenge your own assumptions and remain open to new perspectives.

Active Allyship: Stand in solidarity with marginalized communities by being an active ally. Use your voice to amplify the concerns of people of color, intervene in instances of racism, and support anti-racist policies and practices in your workplace, schools, and communities.

Financial Support: Contribute financially to organizations and initiatives that fight for racial justice. Consider setting up regular donations or participating in fundraising efforts to sustain the vital work being done at the grassroots level.

Civic Engagement: Engage in the political process by voting in local, state, and national elections. Support candidates and policies that promote racial equality. Participate in town hall meetings, join advocacy groups, and use your platform to push for legislative changes.

 Commitments for Communities

Inclusive Community Spaces: Foster inclusive spaces within your community where people of all backgrounds feel welcomed and valued. This can include cultural centers, community gardens, and local events that celebrate diversity and promote cross-cultural understanding.

Community Education Programs: Develop and support education programs that focus on anti-racism, cultural competence, and social justice. Partner with local schools, libraries, and organizations to offer workshops, lectures, and discussion groups.

Support Local Businesses: Encourage your community to support minority-owned businesses. Create directories of local businesses owned by people of color and organize events that highlight their contributions to the community.

Community Advocacy: Form or join local advocacy groups that address specific issues of racism within your community. Work together to identify local problems, develop strategies for addressing them, and advocate for changes at the municipal level.

Commitments for Institutions

Diversity and Inclusion Initiatives: Develop comprehensive diversity and inclusion initiatives that address recruitment, retention, and advancement of people of color. Set measurable goals, track progress, and report on outcomes to ensure accountability.

Equitable Policies: Review and revise institutional policies to ensure they promote equity and do not inadvertently perpetuate discrimination. This includes policies related to hiring, promotions, pay equity, and disciplinary actions.

Cultural Competence Training: Provide ongoing cultural competence and anti-racism training for all employees. Ensure that training is comprehensive, mandatory, and integrated into the institution's core values and practices.

Inclusive Leadership: Promote diversity in leadership positions by implementing mentorship and sponsorship programs for employees of color. Encourage leaders to prioritize equity and inclusion in their decision-making processes.

Commitments for Policymakers

Anti-Racism Legislation: Draft, support, and pass legislation that addresses systemic racism. This includes laws that protect against discrimination in housing, employment, education, and healthcare, as well as policies that address the racial wealth gap.

Criminal Justice Reform: Advocate for comprehensive criminal justice reform that includes ending mass incarceration, eliminating racial profiling, and promoting restorative justice practices. Support policies that ensure accountability for law enforcement and provide alternatives to incarceration.

Equitable Funding: Ensure that public funds are allocated equitably to support marginalized communities. This includes funding for education, healthcare, housing, and economic development programs that directly benefit people of color.

Public Accountability: Create mechanisms for public accountability in government institutions. This can include oversight committees, public reporting requirements, and avenues for community input and feedback on policy decisions.

Collective Actions for Change

Building Coalitions: Form coalitions with other social justice movements to amplify efforts and create a broader impact. Work together to address interconnected issues such as gender inequality, economic disparity, and environmental justice.

Public Awareness Campaigns: Launch public awareness campaigns that educate the broader public about the importance of racial equality. Use various media platforms to disseminate information, share personal stories, and highlight the need for systemic change.

Supporting Youth Activism: Encourage and support youth activism by providing resources, mentorship, and platforms for young leaders to voice their concerns and advocate for change. Youth are often at the forefront of social movements and can drive significant progress.

Global Solidarity: Promote global solidarity in the fight against racism. Support international human rights initiatives, participate in global campaigns, and share best practices across borders to create a united front against racial injustice.

As we reflect on the journey through this book, it is clear that the fight against racism requires sustained effort, collaboration, and a commitment to justice. Each of us has a role to play in this ongoing struggle, and together, we can create a world where racial equality is a reality.

By making individual commitments, fostering inclusive communities, implementing equitable institutional policies, and advocating for systemic change, we can address the root causes of racism and promote a more just and inclusive society. Let us remain vigilant, stay engaged, and continue to support one another in this vital work.

The journey to racial equality is long, but with perseverance, empathy, and collective action, we can achieve a future where everyone is treated with dignity and respect. Let this book be a starting point for further reflection, discussion, and action. Together, we can make a difference and create a better world for future generations.

Reflecting on the themes and discussions throughout this book, it is important to emphasize the transformative power of collective action and sustained commitment. The path to racial equality is challenging and requires the dedication of individuals, communities, and institutions. By taking the insights and strategies discussed, we can work towards a more equitable future.

The Power of Hope and Resilience

Hope and resilience are essential components of the fight against racism. Despite the obstacles and setbacks, maintaining hope and demonstrating resilience can drive the momentum needed for sustained change.

Cultivating Hope: Hope is a powerful motivator. It inspires action and sustains efforts even in the face of adversity. By envisioning a better future and believing in the possibility of change, we can fuel our commitment to the fight against racism. Sharing stories of progress, celebrating successes, and acknowledging the strides made can help cultivate hope.

Building Resilience: Resilience is the ability to withstand and recover from challenges. It is essential in the ongoing fight for racial equality. Building resilience involves fostering strong support networks, practicing self-care, and staying connected to the community. By supporting each other and maintaining a collective strength, we can endure and overcome the challenges we face.

Learning from Setbacks: Setbacks are inevitable in any movement for social change. Rather than becoming discouraged, it is important to learn from these experiences and use them to inform future actions. Reflecting on what went wrong, seeking feedback, and adapting strategies can help strengthen the movement and ensure continued progress.

Engaging the Next Generation

The next generation plays a crucial role in continuing the fight for racial equality. Engaging young people and empowering them with the tools and knowledge to advocate for change is essential for sustaining the momentum.

Education and Empowerment: Providing young people with comprehensive education about racism and social justice is critical. This includes integrating anti-racist curricula in schools, offering workshops and seminars, and creating spaces for youth to discuss and learn about these issues. Empowering youth with knowledge and skills can prepare them to take on leadership roles in the movement.

Mentorship and Support: Mentorship programs that connect young activists with experienced leaders can provide valuable guidance and support. Mentors can share their experiences, offer advice, and help young people navigate the challenges of advocacy work. Supporting youth through mentorship can help build a strong pipeline of future leaders.

Youth-Led Initiatives: Encouraging and supporting youth-led initiatives can amplify their impact and foster innovation. Young people bring fresh perspectives and creative approaches to advocacy. Providing resources, platforms, and opportunities for youth to lead can enhance the movement and drive meaningful change.

A Global Perspective

Racism is a global issue that requires a global response. By understanding the interconnected nature of racial injustices worldwide, we can build solidarity and collaborate across borders to promote racial equality.

International Solidarity: Building international solidarity involves connecting with activists and organizations around the world. Sharing strategies, resources, and experiences can strengthen the global movement for racial justice. International solidarity helps to highlight the commonalities in struggles and fosters a sense of global community.

Learning from Global Movements: Examining successful anti-racist movements in different countries can provide valuable lessons. Understanding how other nations have addressed systemic racism and implemented reforms can inform our strategies and inspire new approaches. By learning from global movements, we can adopt best practices and innovative solutions.

Collaborative Advocacy: Collaborative advocacy across borders can amplify efforts and create broader impact. This involves participating in international campaigns, supporting global human rights initiatives, and advocating for policies that promote racial equality worldwide. Collaborative advocacy ensures that the fight against racism is comprehensive and inclusive.

Sustaining the Momentum

Sustaining the momentum in the fight against racism requires ongoing effort, dedication, and a willingness to adapt and evolve. By staying committed and continuously pushing for progress, we can ensure that the movement remains strong and effective.

Continuous Engagement: Staying engaged in the fight against racism means continuously educating oneself, participating in advocacy efforts, and supporting marginalized communities. It involves making anti-racism a core part of one's values and actions.

Adapting to Change: The landscape of social justice is constantly evolving. Being open to change, adapting strategies, and embracing new ideas are essential for sustaining the momentum. Flexibility and innovation can help address emerging challenges and seize new opportunities for progress.

Building Long-Term Alliances: Building long-term alliances with other social justice movements can strengthen the fight against racism. These alliances can provide support, share resources, and collaborate on joint initiatives. Long-term alliances ensure that efforts are sustained, and that the movement remains resilient.

Personal Commitment

Every individual has the power to make a difference. Personal commitment to fighting racism begins with self-awareness and extends to everyday actions that promote equity and inclusion.

Self-Reflection and Growth: Regularly reflect on your own beliefs, biases, and behaviours. Acknowledge the privileges you may have and understand how they impact your perspectives. Commit to continuous learning and personal growth by engaging with diverse viewpoints and educating yourself about racism and its effects.

Taking Responsibility: Accept responsibility for your role in perpetuating or challenging racism. This includes speaking out against racist comments, behaviours, and policies, and supporting those who are marginalized. Your actions, no matter how small, contribute to the broader fight for justice.

Practicing Empathy: Cultivate empathy by listening to and understanding the experiences of others. Empathy allows us to connect on a human level and fosters a deeper commitment to advocating for those who face discrimination and injustice.

Collective Responsibility

Collective responsibility involves working together to create systemic change. By collaborating with others, we can amplify our efforts and achieve greater impact.

Building Alliances: Form alliances with individuals and organizations that share a commitment to racial justice. Collaborative efforts can pool resources, share knowledge, and strengthen advocacy. Building alliances also creates a support network that can sustain momentum and resilience in the face of challenges.

Community Engagement: Engage with your community to address local issues of racism. This can involve organizing events, participating in community meetings, and supporting local initiatives that promote equity. Community engagement helps create a sense of collective responsibility and fosters a culture of inclusion.

Advocating for Policy Change: Advocate for policies that promote racial equality at the local, state, and national levels. This includes supporting legislation that addresses systemic racism, holding policymakers accountable, and participating in advocacy campaigns. Policy change is essential for creating lasting and meaningful impact.

Sustaining the Movement

Sustaining the movement for racial equality requires ongoing effort, dedication, and adaptability. By remaining committed and resilient, we can continue to make progress towards a more just society.

Long-Term Vision: Maintain a long-term vision for racial equality. Recognize that this is an ongoing journey that requires sustained effort over time. Celebrate the milestones achieved but remain focused on the ultimate goal of dismantling systemic racism.

Resilience in the Face of Adversity: Expect setbacks and challenges along the way. Building resilience involves staying committed to the cause, learning from failures, and finding strength in the collective effort. Resilience is essential for sustaining the movement and overcoming obstacles.

Adapting Strategies: Be open to adapting strategies as the landscape of social justice evolves. This includes embracing new technologies, learning from other movements, and being flexible in your approaches. Adaptability ensures that efforts remain relevant and effective.

A Shared Commitment to Justice

The fight for racial equality is a shared commitment that requires each of us to play our part. By working together, we can create a more inclusive and equitable world for future generations.

Inspiring Others: Use your platform and influence to inspire others to join the fight against racism. Share your journey, highlight the importance of racial justice, and encourage those around you to take action. Inspiring others can create a ripple effect that amplifies the impact of the movement.

Supporting Future Leaders: Invest in the next generation of leaders by providing mentorship, resources, and opportunities for growth. Supporting future leaders ensures that the movement for racial equality continues and evolves. Encourage young people to take on leadership roles and empower them to drive change.

Celebrating Diversity: Embrace and celebrate diversity in all its forms. Recognize the value that different perspectives, experiences, and cultures bring to our communities. Celebrating diversity fosters a sense of belonging and strengthens the fabric of our society.

Final Reflections

As we conclude this book, I want to express my gratitude for your commitment to this journey. The fight against racism is not easy, but it is necessary. Together, we can create a world where everyone is treated with dignity and respect, where equity and inclusion are the norms, and where racial equality is a reality for all.

Let this book be a starting point for further reflection, discussion, and action. Draw strength from the resilience of those who have come before us and those who continue to fight for justice. Let us move forward with hope, resilience, and a shared commitment to creating a better world.

It is important to remember that the fight against racism is a collective endeavor that requires the participation of everyone. By taking the insights and strategies discussed and committing to action, we can create a more just and inclusive society.

Let us draw inspiration from the resilience and strength of those who have come before us and those who continue to fight for justice today. Together, we can make a difference and build a world where racial equality is a reality for all.

Thank you for embarking on this journey with me. Let us move forward with hope, resilience, and a shared commitment to justice.

In this final reflection, I want to emphasize the importance of personal commitment and the collective responsibility we all share in the journey towards racial equality. This concluding chapter is a call to action for everyone to take tangible steps to dismantle racism and build a more inclusive and just world.

Epilogue

As I reflect on the journey of writing this book, I am reminded of the profound significance of our collective efforts to combat racism and promote equality. This book is not just a collection of pages filled with historical accounts, personal reflections, and strategies for change. It is a call to action, a testament to the resilience of marginalized communities, and a beacon of hope for a more inclusive future.

The journey to racial equality is a marathon, not a sprint. It requires perseverance, continuous learning, and unwavering commitment. Throughout history, we have witnessed both tremendous progress and heartbreaking setbacks. The fight against racism is complex and multifaceted, involving not only policy changes and institutional reforms but also deep introspection and personal transformation.

The Importance of Storytelling

Throughout this book, we have explored the power of storytelling. Stories have the ability to humanize abstract concepts, bridge divides, and foster empathy. They remind us that behind every statistic and policy debate are real people with real experiences. By sharing these stories, we honour the struggles and triumphs of those who have fought for justice and inspire others to join the movement.

A Call for Continuous Action

This book is a starting point, not an end. The strategies
and actions outlined in these pages are meant to guide
and inspire, but the real work happens beyond these
words. It happens in our daily lives, in the choices we
make, and in the actions we take. Each of us has a role to
play, and every effort, no matter how small, contributes
to the broader movement for racial justice.

Gratitude and Acknowledgments

I am deeply grateful to all the individuals and
communities who have shared their stories, insights, and
experiences with me. Your courage and resilience are the
foundation of this book. I also extend my heartfelt thanks
to the countless activists, educators, and leaders who
have dedicated their lives to the fight for equality. Your
work paves the way for future generations.

A Vision for the Future

As we look to the future, let us do so with a sense of
hope and determination. Imagine a world where racial
equality is not an aspiration but a reality. A world where
every individual is valued for their unique contributions,
where diversity is celebrated, and where justice prevails.
This vision is within our reach, but it requires all of us to
work together.

Moving Forward

I encourage you to carry the lessons and insights from this book into your everyday life. Engage in conversations about race, support anti-racist initiatives, and continue to educate yourself and others. Let this book be a catalyst for action, a source of inspiration, and a reminder that together, we can create a more just and equitable world.

Thank you for joining me on this journey. The road ahead may be challenging, but it is one we must travel together. Let us move forward with courage, compassion, and a steadfast commitment to justice. Together, we can build a future where racial equality is not just a goal but a lived reality for all.

With hope and solidarity,

Dr Bhaskar Bora

References

Alexander, M. (2010). The New Jim Crow: Mass Incarceration in the Age of Colorblindness. New York: The New Press.

Anzaldúa, G. (1987). Borderlands/La Frontera: The New Mestiza. San Francisco: Aunt Lute Books.

Berlin, I. (1998). Many Thousands Gone: The First Two Centuries of Slavery in North America. Cambridge, MA: Harvard University Press.

Bonilla-Silva, E. (2003). Racism Without Racists: Color-Blind Racism and the Persistence of Racial Inequality in the United States. Lanham, MD: Rowman & Littlefield Publishers.

Coates, T. N. (2015). Between the World and Me. New York: Spiegel & Grau.

Crenshaw, K. (1995). Critical Race Theory: The Key Writings that Formed the Movement. New York: The New Press.

Davis, D. B. (2006). Inhuman Bondage: The Rise and Fall of Slavery in the New World. New York: Oxford University Press.

DiAngelo, R. (2018). White Fragility: Why It's So Hard for White People to Talk About Racism. Boston: Beacon Press.

Eddo-Lodge, R. (2017). Why I'm No Longer Talking to White People About Race. London: Bloomsbury Publishing.

Fanon, F. (1961). The Wretched of the Earth. New York: Grove Press.

Feagin, J. R. (2014). Racist America: Roots, Current Realities, and Future Reparations. 3rd ed. New York: Routledge.

Fredrickson, G. M. (2002). Racism: A Short History. Princeton, NJ: Princeton University Press.

Freire, P. (1970). Pedagogy of the Oppressed. New York: Continuum.

Gilroy, P. (2002). There Ain't No Black in the Union Jack: The Cultural Politics of Race and Nation. 2nd ed. London: Routledge.

Hannaford, I. (1996). Race: The History of an Idea in the West. Washington, D.C.: Woodrow Wilson Center Press.

Harris, F. C. (2014). The Next American Revolution: Sustainable Activism for the Twenty-First Century. Berkeley, CA: University of California Press.

hooks, b. (2000). All About Love: New Visions. New York: William Morrow Paperbacks.

hooks, b. (2000). Where We Stand: Class Matters. New York: Routledge.

Kendi, I. X. (2019). How to Be an Antiracist. New York: One World.

Kivel, P. (2017). Uprooting Racism: How White People Can Work for Racial Justice. 4th ed. Gabriola Island, BC: New Society Publishers.

Loury, G. C. (2008). Race, Incarceration, and American Values. Cambridge, MA: MIT Press.

McIntosh, P. (1988). White Privilege and Male Privilege: A Personal Account of Coming to See Correspondences through Work in Women's Studies. Wellesley, MA: Wellesley College Center for Research on Women.

Omi, M., & Winant, H. (2014). Racial Formation in the United States. 3rd ed. New York: Routledge.

Steyn, M. (2001). Whiteness Just Isn't What It Used to Be: White Identity in a Changing South Africa. Albany, NY: SUNY Press.

Sue, D. W. (2010). Microaggressions in Everyday Life: Race, Gender, and Sexual Orientation. Hoboken, NJ: Wiley.

Tatum, B. D. (1997). "Why Are All the Black Kids Sitting Together in the Cafeteria?" And Other Conversations About Race. New York: Basic Books.

Copyright Information

Disclaimer

The information contained in this book is for general informational purposes only. The author has made every effort to ensure the accuracy and completeness of the information provided but assumes no responsibility for errors or omissions. The reader is advised to verify any information before relying on it.

The views and opinions expressed in this book are those of the author and do not necessarily reflect the official policy or position of any other agency, organization, employer, or company. The author is not responsible for, and expressly disclaims all liability for, damages of any kind arising out of the use, reference to, or reliance on any information contained within the book.

Legal Notice

The author and publisher have made every effort to
ensure that the information in this book was correct at
the time of publication. The author and publisher do not
assume and hereby disclaim any liability to any party for
any loss, damage, or disruption caused by errors or
omissions, whether such errors or omissions result from
negligence, accident, or any other cause.

Trademarks

All trademarks, service marks, trade names, and trade
dress used in this book are the property of their
respective owners. The use of any trade name or
trademark is for identification and reference purposes
only and does not imply any association with the
trademark holder or their brand.

Fair Use Notice

This book may contain copyrighted material, the use of
which has not always been specifically authorized by the
copyright owner. The author is making such material
available in an effort to advance understanding of issues
of racism, social justice, and equity. This constitutes a
'fair use' of any such copyrighted material as provided
for in section 107 of the US Copyright Law. In
accordance with Title 17 U.S.C. Section 107, the
material in this book is distributed without profit to those
who have expressed a prior interest in receiving the

included information for research and educational purposes.

Acknowledgments

The author wishes to acknowledge and thank all those whose works have contributed to the research and insights shared in this book. While every effort has been made to credit sources accurately, any errors or omissions are unintentional and will be corrected in future editions upon notification.

Contact Information

For inquiries, permissions, or further information, please contact:

Dr Bhaskar Bora
bora.dr@gmail.com